Australian Wildflowers in Stumpwork

Australian Wildflowers in Stumpwork

Annette Hinde

Kangaroo Press

Acknowledgments

This book would not have been written without the encouragement and support of some special people I know.

I would like to say a special thank you to:

My husband Denis and four children, Jack, Scott, Steven and Alice, who have been very encouraging and understanding while I have stitched and typed.

My friends Garry, Nerida and Kerry, who have read the typed pages and corrected the many spelling mistakes.

My sister Pam, who was able to tell me if my instructions were clear and readable.

My brother Bruce, who gave technical advice on how to use a computer.

Alan Barker for taking such wonderful photos.

Jennifer Kime for allowing me to photograph her butterfly box.

My editor Anne Savage.

Cover: *Waratah with Insects embroidery from page 75.*

Frontispiece: *This posy of wildflowers, my favourite, is worked on a cream poly satin fabric. I have taught it many times and enjoyed sharing the techniques with many wonderful people (see page 69).*

Australian Wildflowers in Stumpwork

First published in Australia in 1999 by Kangaroo Press
an imprint of Simon & Schuster Australia
20 Barcoo Street, East Roseville NSW 2069

Reprinted in 1999

A Viacom Company
Sydney New York London Toronto Tokyo Singapore

© Annette Hinde 1999

National Library of Australia
Cataloguing-in-Publication data

Hinde, Annette.
Australian wildflowers in stumpwork.

Bibliography.
Includes index.
ISBN 0 86417 883 2.

1. Stump work. I. Title.
746.44

Photographer: Alan Barker

Set in Perpetua 10.5/13
Printed in Hong Kong and produced by Phoenix Offset

10 9 8 7 6 5 4 3 2

Contents

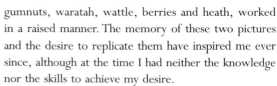ntroduction

THE INITIAL INSPIRATION for these dimensional Australian native flower embroideries came during a holiday visit to the Queen Victoria Museum and Art Gallery in Launceston, Tasmania, in 1986. Hanging in the museum were two beautiful embroideries of Australian native flowers featuring gum blossom and

gumnuts, waratah, wattle, berries and heath, worked in a raised manner. The memory of these two pictures and the desire to replicate them have inspired me ever since, although at the time I had neither the knowledge nor the skills to achieve my desire.

Over the following years I attended classes with the Embroiderer's Guild of New South Wales, progressing through the basic embroidery course and the intermediate certificate as well as a number of other workshops. During this time I was introduced to stumpwork (raised embroidery) through slides shown by Ann Baker and to practical stitching in a stumpwork class led by Pat Langford. Further reading and research and a class with Jane Nicholas provided me with the skills and confidence to reproduce the type of embroidery I had seen so many years before. Following the advice of a visiting English tutor, 'to embroider only what you can see or hold', I looked around my own garden and used the native plants growing there as a template for my first embroideries. My first effort was fluffy wattle, and I rapidly moved on to new adventures.

As my skills developed I began to teach my methods of creating dimensional embroideries to embroiderers' groups in New South Wales, the ACT and Queensland. Sharing what I had discovered with other stitchers meant that some of my techniques were refined and other methods of creating naturalistic raised flowers were discussed.

Unknown, Tasmania: Eucalyptus leaves and flowers, 1890s. Silk and linen on velvet, 500 x 395 mm.
Collection: Queen Victoria Museum and Art Gallery, Launceston, Tasmania. Photographer: John Leeming

Unknown, Tasmania: Floral bouquet, possibly late 19th century.
Wool, linen and silk on linen, 594 x 552 mm.
Donated by: Mr and Mrs A.D. Mackay.

Collection: Queen Victoria Museum and Art Gallery, Launceston,
Tasmania. Photographer: John Leeming

People in my classes showed me examples of 'wattle work' that their families had held onto over the years and I started searching in books and museums for other examples of raised embroideries.

The Embroiderer's Guild of New South Wales have in their collection a tea cosy made in Wagga Wagga over one hundred years ago that features wattle, flannel flowers and waratah. Also included in their collection is a framed picture featuring a basket of native flowers and insects. The picture has 'For Mum' embroidered into it as well as the date, 14–12–04. Both samples feature chenille threads, wattle balls made of wool and flannel flowers made from velvet or pile fabric glued onto paper or card; the petal shapes were cut out and attached to the embroidery.

Some years later, after developing my own techniques, I went back to Tasmania to look again at my original source of inspiration. When I saw the embroideries again, I realised they were much larger than I had remembered and were worked in thicker threads than I had been using—wool, chenille threads of varying thicknesses, linen and silk threads. They also had a lot of flat embroidery areas and a few raised sections.

This second visit has led to the realisation that further research is needed to answer the many questions now forming in my mind. The few facts I have are not much to work with, although there are many surviving examples of raised Australian native flower embroideries in museums in Tasmania. They take different forms—framed pictures, shelf runners, table cloths and lambrequins (drapes hung from the mantelpiece). There is a church screen made up of four panels, two featuring raised work and two with appliqué (embroidered by Sarah E. Mitchell, dated 1879).

Little information is available about the majority of these pieces. In most cases we do not know who worked them or which families donated them to the museums. Examination reveals many similarities in the types of threads used and the way in which the flat embroidery and raised elements were worked. Some of the workmanship is of a very high standard, while other pieces are amateurish in their execution. Mrs Amelia Burgess exhibited her embroidery as part of the Tasmanian contribution to the Universal Exhibition of Industry in Paris in 1885. The embroidery represented native flowers of Tasmania taken from nature.

It has been well documented that Tasmanian female artists followed the examples of Mary Morton Allport and Louisa Ann Meredith and painted the flowers and insects of the Tasmanian countryside, but I have found no evidence of the possible source of inspiration for those early Tasmanian embroiderers. Could one of the artists of the time have designed the embroideries, or could a leading embroiderer of the time have designed and worked an embroidery, then taught others her methods? It is also possible that there was a published source of the designs and a retail outlet for the supplies. The designs used on the mantelshelf runners are stylistically the same as those printed in the *English Women's Domestic Magazine* and *The Young Ladies Journal* in the late 1880s, with Australian native flowers replacing the English flowers. The same types of threads have been used in both designs.

I would like to thank Glenda King from the Queen Victoria Museum and Art Gallery in Launceston, Allison Melrose from the Tasmanian Museum and Art Gallery, Hobart, and the staff at Narryna Folk Museum for showing me their collections and sharing their information on this subject.

My next goal is to find out more about the designers and the people who worked these embroideries in Tasmania during the late 1800s and early 1900s. The only written instructions I have been able to find are in a book by Mrs Lance Rawson, *The Australian Enquiry Book of Household and General Information* of 1894. This gives instruction for wattle work and flannel flowers.

In my book I have detailed the techniques that I have adapted to work these raised embroideries. The scope for variation to the techniques I have used or for different approaches to create the raised effect is limited only by time and imagination.

Although the act of creating and stitching can at times be very frustrating, in the end it always brings me a sense of peace and contentment and pleasure.

Happy stitching.

Annette Hinde
'Kelmar' 1999

Part 1

Techniques and Stitches

Chapter One

MATERIALS AND BASIC TECHNIQUES

Fabrics

I use a sandwich of three layers of different fabrics as the background for my raised embroidery.

The *backing fabric* is a firm natural fibre fabric such as calico, homespun or quilter's muslin. The design outline is traced onto this fabric, which forms the underside of the fabric sandwich.

For the second layer of the sandwich I use *pelon* or a *thin wadding fabric*. This layer is included to absorb the thickness of the wire used in the embroidery and the ends of the threads. It also provides an extra dimension to the embroidery, giving a quilted look to the stitches worked on the surface.

The visible *background (surface) fabric* on which the stitches are worked can be any fabric that you wish. The seventeenth century embroiderers used fine linen canvas or ivory-coloured silk, while the naturalistic wildflower embroideries done in Tasmania at the end of the nineteenth century were worked on dark coloured velvets (red, olive-green, black), and on twill weave fabrics, possibly wool/linen mixtures or heavy cottons or satin.

I have worked many of my projects on a poly satin fabric in a cream colour. Embroiderers using velvet fabric as a background may find that the threads tend to sink into the pile; in this case you will need to increase the number of strands of thread you use.

Scissors

To complete the projects you will need:
- Large scissors for cutting out the fabrics
- Small embroidery scissors for cutting thread
- Small sharp, pointed scissors for cutting around wired shapes
- Craft scissors for cutting felt and wire (never cut wire with your good embroidery scissors)

Embroidery hoop

Any raised embroidery must be kept taut in some kind of hoop or frame until the work has been completed. A 20, 25 or 30 cm (8", 10" or 12") round hoop is all that will be required to work any of the projects in this book. Larger projects than these may need to be laced onto a frame.

The hoop you choose can affect the finish you will achieve in your embroidery. If you are using a wooden hoop, choose the kind with an outer ring that can be tightened with a screwdriver. Make sure the wood feels smooth on your fingers.

Plastic hoops are available, in which the inner hoop has a rim that holds the fabric firmly when the outer hoop is screwed into position.

For working detached slips a 10 cm (4") wooden, plastic or ring hoop is all that is required.

A special frame that fixes a hoop to the edge of a table, or a hoop stand, can be a definite advantage, as they free both hands to work on the embroidery. Set at the right height, these stands can help minimise the risk of the embroiderer's curse—tired, stiff neck and back.

Needles

I often say in class that it could have been a needle manufacturer who introduced the concept of raised embroidery! To work these projects you will need needles in a variety of sizes and types—crewel, chenille and tapestry needles are all used. To stitch over wire I like to use a hand appliqué 12 needle. For attaching detached wired shapes I use a yarn darning needle.

Threads

I admit to being a threadaholic—but for the projects in this book I have tried to stay with threads that I hope are easy to obtain.

Most of the embroidery is worked using DMC stranded cottons. For thicker threads I have used DMC perle threads in various thicknesses.

In the padding stitches I have used DMC no.4 soft cotton. For achieving special effects I have made use of Cifonda silk threads, machine rayon and metallic threads.

Wire

The wires I use in these projects are available from cake decorating suppliers.

♦ 30 gauge cotton covered wire: This comes in a variety of colours. White cotton covered wire can be coloured with watercolour paint or pencil if required.

♦ 30 gauge paper covered wire: This is finer in diameter than the cotton covered wire and can also be coloured if you wish.

♦ 34 gauge beading wire: This wire is uncovered but it is very fine and most suitable to use on the butterfly wings.

♦ Fine silk covered wire (diameters 0.01" and 0.012") is also suitable for insect wings and the veins of petals.

♦ Fuse wire and the wire from inside electrical cord may also be used.

Beads

Mill Hill glass beads come in a wide range of colours and are suitable for details such as insects' eyes. Choose from the seed bead or petite seed bead ranges, depending on the size you want.

Glue

Some projects make use of glue. I use white PVA glue available from supermarkets, craft shops and hardware shops.

The wildflower posy from page 69 as a work in progress. There are three layers of fabric in the hoop, and the flat embroidery has been completed. Surrounding the flat embroidery are all the completed detached components ready to be attached.

Other bits and pieces

A screwdriver to tighten the screw on the embroidery hoop can be useful.

Small fine pliers are essential for bending the wire shapes.

Tweezers are very useful for bending wire and for arranging the detached shapes after you have attached them to your work.

Transferring a design

Raised embroidery has the disadvantage that it cannot be washed or cleaned when the project has been completed. Thus, it is to the stitcher's advantage to have as few marks as possible on the front of the work.

To overcome this problem and the problem of transferring the design onto dark fabrics I have devised the following method: First trace the design outline onto tracing paper with a black pen. Then lay the tracing on a light box or use masking tape to fix it to a window pane. (The window method can only be used in daylight.) Place the backing fabric (calico/homespun/quilter's muslin) over the design so that the design outline is in the centre. Use a B pencil to trace the design onto the fabric.

The design outline is the reverse image of the picture you are working.

Putting fabric into the hoop

On a firm surface (table), place the background fabric right side down. On top of it place the square of pelon, then the square of backing fabric with the design outline drawing facing you.

Lay the inner ring of the hoop on top of the fabric sandwich so the design is in the centre. Carefully turn the inner hoop and fabrics over and press the outer hoop over the fabrics. Tighten the hoop so that the fabric is taut.

You may need to pull on the fabric to get it taut. This can be done by placing the hoop on a table with the background fabric face down on the table and pulling on the edges of the calico all around the hoop. Turn the hoop over so that the background fabric is facing you and the hoop is partly over the edge of the table. Pull down on the edges of the background fabric, right around the edge of the hoop, while turning it.

> **TIP:** The fabric must stay tight in the hoop or on the frame until the project is complete.

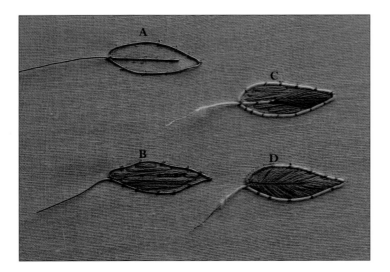

Transferring the design to the front

Working from the back, i.e. with the backing fabric and design outline facing you, work a running stitch along the traced lines, using 1 strand of stranded cotton in the colours specified in the requirements list for the project.

The running stitch is worked with a stabbing action along the pencil line. Make the stitches facing you 5 mm (¼") long and the stitches on the right side of the work much smaller, about 2 mm (⅛") long Take the needle through all the fabric layers, always at right angles to the fabric.

The design will appear as small running stitches on the right side of your work.

Slips

Slips are detached pieces which are embroidered on calico or homespun fabric and attached to the surface of the embroidery after all the flat embroidery has been completed. They are not free of the embroidery like wired shapes, and often have padding under them to give them a more raised up appearance.

Cutting out and attaching slips

When the slip has been embroidered, use doubled machine thread to work running stitches around the shape about 2 mm (⅛") out from the embroidery. Do not end off the running stitch. Use a small brush to paint PVA glue outside the running stitches, taking care not to get glue on them. When the glue is dry, cut out the slip around the glue line. Pull up the running stitches so that the excess fabric folds under the embroidered shape. Position the slip on the surface of the embroidery and attach with slip stitch.

Detached embroidered wired shapes

Detached embroidered wired shapes are used for leaves and flower petals which stand above the embroidery, with the wire giving them strength and stability. The leaf shown in the photograph illustrates the technique.

Stages in making a detached embroidered wired shape.
A Couch wire down the centre and around the shape
B Fill inside wired shape with long straight stitches
C Use your chosen filling stitch to fill inside the wired shape
D Work satin stitch or buttonhole stitch over the wire
The shape can now be cut out and attached to the embroidery

1. The shape is traced onto washed calico, quilter's muslin or homespun. If the shape is less than 2 cm (¾") square, a firm interfacing may be used in place of the calico, quilter's muslin or homespun. Interfacing's greatest advantage is that it leaves no frayed edges after cutting.

2. The next step is to couch the wire along the shape outline (A). For this, use a hand appliqué needle and a single strand of stranded cotton. Bring the needle and thread up inside the shape, close to the wire, and then take them down on the outside of the shape, again close to the wire. The needle should always be at right angles to the fabric when entering and leaving it. Give the thread a bit of a tug as you bring it up through the fabric. Couching stitches are spaced about 3–5 mm apart (¹/₈"–¼").

3. The inside of the wired shape is filled with padding in the form of straight stitches (B). If you are using stranded cotton, the threads should be separated and put together again before threading the needle. Work the stitches along the length of the shape, and side by side, never in the same direction as the top filling stitches.

4. Fill inside the shape with your chosen filling stitch (C), bringing the needle up and down as close to the inside of the wire as possible.

5. Using a single strand of thread, work a row of satin stitch or close buttonhole stitch around the shape over the wire (D). In satin stitch bring the needle up inside the embroidery close to the wire, and take it down on the outside of the wired shape. If you are using buttonhole stitch, place the loops on the outside of the wired shape

Cutting out detached wired shapes

Use sharp pointed scissors or nail scissors for cutting out detached wired shapes.

Remove the embroidered shape from the hoop. Pull the fabric away from the edge of the wired shape. Hold the embroidered fabric firmly over your index finger with your thumb and other fingers, with the right side of the embroidery facing you and the edge to be cut at the top of the finger.

Slip the point of the scissors into the fabric close to the stitching and cut the free fabric away as close to the stitch line as possible.

TIP: Try to angle the scissors so that the lower blade is just under the embroidery and the upper (visible) blade is tilted away from the embroidery.

Holding the fabric as firmly as possible, move it over your finger as you continue cutting right around the shape.

Turn the shape over so the wrong side is facing you and run your finger along the cut edge to raise any frayed bits. Cut them away. The shape is now ready to be attached to the embroidery.

TIP: If you cut the embroidery don't panic—just paint the cut thread with a little PVA glue and allow to dry before continuing.

TIP: To further disguise the furry cut edges, moisten a water-soluble pencil of an appropriate colour and wipe it around the shape.

Attaching a detached wired shape

1. Using a large yarn darning needle, push the needle through the background fabric so that its eye is visible above and below the fabric (Fig. 1a).

2. Slip any threads that are wrapped around the wire through the eye of the needle (Fig. 1b).

3. Poke the end of the wire through the hole created by the eye of the needle and pull the wire down through the hole (Fig. 1c).

4. Stand the wired shape at right angles to the background fabric and fold the wire so it lies in the same direction that the embroidered shape will sit.

5. Stitch the wire in position with a single strand of thread; in most cases the wire can be stitched down with three or four satin stitches, using a thread that matches the background fabric. Take the thread up and down through all the layers of fabric, close to where the wire enters the fabric.

6. Fold the shape down into its final position.

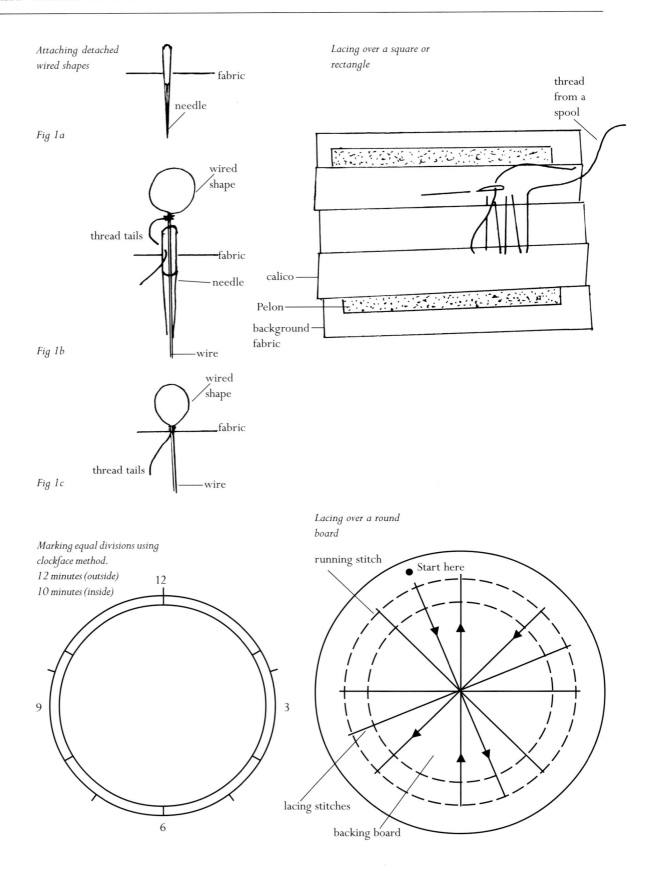

Attaching detached
wired shapes

fabric

needle

Fig 1a

wired
shape

thread tails

fabric

needle

Fig 1b

wire

wired
shape

fabric

thread tails

Fig 1c

wire

Lacing over a square or
rectangle

thread
from a
spool

calico

Pelon

background
fabric

Marking equal divisions using
clockface method.
12 minutes (outside)
10 minutes (inside)

12

9

3

6

Lacing over a round
board

running stitch

Start here

lacing stitches

backing board

Bonded fabrics

Fabric shapes may be bonded onto the background to form leaves.

Trace the required shape onto fusible web (Vliesofix).

Lay an appliqué mat or Gladbake on the ironing board, then the fusible web, the fabric which has been cut slightly larger than the fusible web and cover with an appliqué mat or Gladbake.

Use a dry iron on a temperature suitable for the fabric you are using.

Press the iron down on the sandwich of materials you have on the ironing board. Hold the iron down for 5 to 10 seconds. Do not move the iron around.

Cut out the required shape and remove any paper backing.

Position the shape on the background fabric. Cover the background fabric and the shape with the appliqué mat or Gladbake and bond in place with the tip of the iron. Hold the iron tip against the shape for 5 to 10 seconds.

Fabrics in the appropriate colours may be used to make raised wired leaves or petal shapes.

To create wired fabric shapes bond two pieces of the fabric together with fusible web (Vliesofix). Place the bonded fabric in a hoop and stitch wire around the outer edge and/or down the centre of the shape.

Remove from the hoop and cut out the shape in the same way as an embroidered wired shape.

Marking equal divisions around a circle

This is simple to do if you imagine a clock face. Following the diagram:

To mark five equal spaces around a circle, place pencil marks at 12 o'clock, 12 minutes, 24 minutes, 36 minutes and 48 minutes past the hour (60 minutes ÷ 5 = 12 minutes).

To mark six equal spaces the pencil marks are placed at 10 minute intervals around the clock face (60 minutes ÷ 6 = 10 minutes).

Mounting work

To be able to take your work to the framer already backed and ready for framing is a very satisfying feeling. It is not hard to do.

When an embroidery is completed to your satisfaction you can take it out of its hoop or frame—but not before.

Cut backing board to the appropriate size; you can use foam core board, box board or a piece of 3 mm craftwood. Smooth the edges of the board with sandpaper.

Lay the embroidery, embroidered face down, into an open box or other container which is smaller than the backing board, with an opening larger than the embroidered surface. Place the backing board over the embroidery. Fold the free edges of fabric over and stick down onto the back of the board with masking tape. Turn the embroidery over and make sure the motif is centred on the backing board. Make any adjustment needed.

Lay the embroidery face down over the opening of the box again. Remove the masking tape, taking care not to move the fabrics too much.

Lace the edges of the calico (base) layer of fabric together over the board in a criss-cross pattern. If the shape is rectangular lace the long sides together first, then the short sides.

> **TIP:** If you do not like lacing, PVA glue or staples can be used, but remember to allow the glue to dry on each side before going on to the next side. At this stage check the work is correctly centred and make any adjustments needed.

Cut away the layer of pelon, leaving it 5 mm (¼") larger than the backing board, then firmly lace, glue or staple the background (surface) fabric to the backing board, attaching the short sides first, then the long sides.

Lacing round shapes

Position the backing board on the wrong side of the embroidery and pencil around the shape. Work a row of running stitch in the calico only, about 3 cm (1¼") from the pencil line, using Perle 5 thread. Trim away the excess fabric and position the mounting board. Pull up the running stitch firmly and end it off.

Cut the pelon so it is 3 mm ($^1/_8$") larger than the mounting board. Repeat the running stitch step on the background fabric.

Following the diagram work lacing stitches around the circle to hold the embroidery firmly.

Turn the embroidery face up and use tweezers to arrange the raised shapes before taking it to the framer.

Chapter Two

STITCH INSTRUCTIONS

ALL THE STITCHES used in my raised embroideries are worked as stabbed stitches. This means that putting the needle and thread down into the fabric, and bringing them up out of the fabric, are two separate actions. Stitches are worked this way because the fabric must be stretched tight in the hoop at all times. If you are not used to working in a hoop it may take a little time to get used to the stab action.

The threads can be anchored in the backing fabric; I prefer not to use knots in my work, although there is no hard and fast rule about this. Try to anchor threads under areas that will be embroidered.

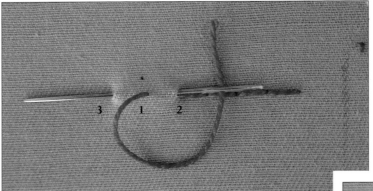

Backstitch

Worked from right to left. Bring needle and thread out at 1 and back into the fabric to the right of 1, at 2. Bring the needle and thread out again at 3, to the left of 1.

Left-handed stitchers work from right to left, i.e. 2 will be to the left of 1, and 3 will be to the right.

Whipped backstitch

Work a row of backstitch. Thread the whipping thread into a tapestry needle. The needle and thread pass between the backstitch and the fabric, not entering the fabric except to begin and end the whipping.

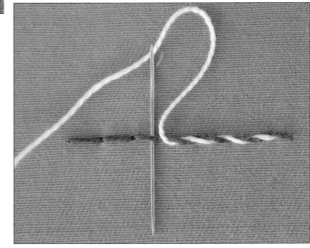

Bullion stitch

Take the needle up through the fabric at 1, down at 2, the required length of the finished bullion, and up again at 1, only part way through the fabric. Leave most of the thread on the right side of the work.

Wrap the thread around the needle in a clockwise direction, the number of wraps depending on the length of the first stitch.

Take the needle down through the fabric at 2 and pull up the thread to tighten the wraps.

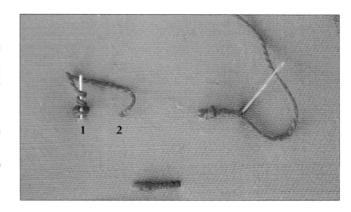

Buttonhole stitch

Worked from left to right with the loops towards you.

Left-handed stitchers work right to left with the loops away from you.

This is a looped stitch. To start, bring the thread out along the line the loops will be on. Take straight downward stitches from above this line, keeping the thread under the point of the needle. Pull up the stitch.

The thread is under the needle when it comes out at 2.

Chain stitch

Worked from the top of the work to the bottom, the thread looped under the needle. Bring the needle out on the line, hold the thread down and insert the needle where it came out. Bring the point of the needle out a short distance down the line, keeping the thread under the needle point. Pull the stitch up.

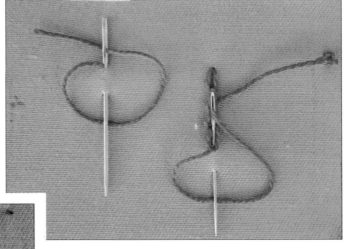

Detached chain stitch (lazy daisy stitch)

Each stitch is anchored with a tie-down stitch.

Whipped chain stitch

Work a row of chain stitch. Thread the whipping thread into a tapestry needle. Needle and thread pass between the fabric and the chain stitch. Go under both arms of the chain stitch.

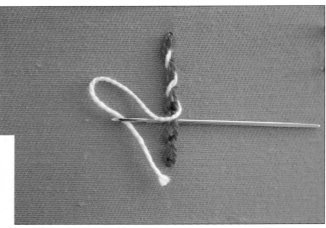

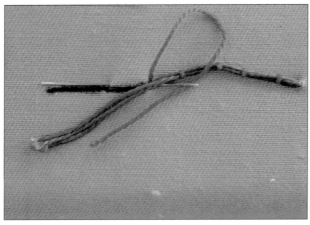

Couching

The thread is laid along the design line. Thread a needle with another thread and use small stitches to attach the laid thread to the fabric. Bring the needle and thread up on the design line over the laid thread and down through the fabric on the design line.

Cut turkey stitch

Worked from left to right. The stitch is a series of stitches made up of a looped stitch then a flat stitch. *Left-handed stitchers* work from right to left. I suggest you turn the diagrams on the next page upside down.

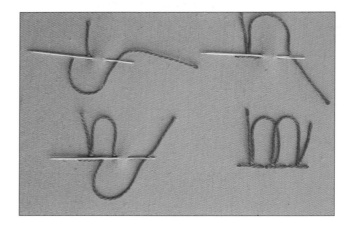

Following the numbers on the diagrams, take the needle and thread in from the front (1), leaving a tail of thread on the surface of the work. Bring the thread up to the left of this point (2).

Pulling the thread towards you, take the needle down to the right of where you first went down (3). This is a flat stitch.

Bring the needle and thread up close to where you first went down (4).

Pulling the thread away from you, take the needle and thread down to the right of the last stitch (5). This is a looped stitch.

Bring the needle and thread up at the end of the last stitch (3). Take the needle and thread down to the right of the last stitch (6). This is a flat stitch.

Cut turkey stitch

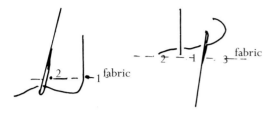

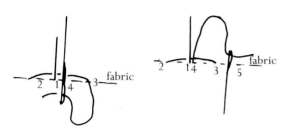

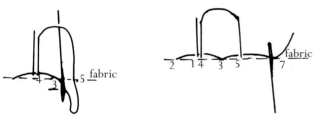

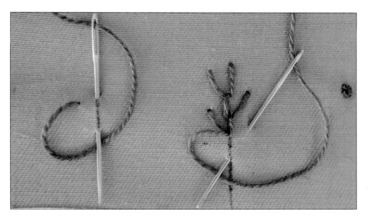

Fishbone stitch

Anchor the thread along the vein line with small back-stitches.

Bring needle out at 1 and down at 2 at the top of the shape.

Bring the needle up to the right and a thread width down from the first stitch (3). Cross the thread over the first stitch and take the needle and thread down on the left of the first stitch (4).

The stitches are made so they alternate from one side to another. Each time you make a stitch travel a further thread width down the centre and side of the shape.

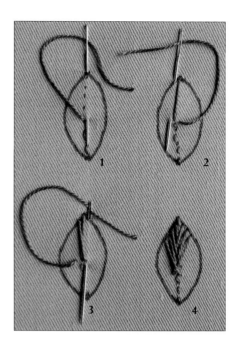

Feather stitch

Worked from top to bottom. Bring the needle out on the line. Holding the thread down with your thumb, insert the needle to the left of where you came up and take a small stitch to the centre line. Keep the thread under the needle point. Pull up the thread.

The next stitch is formed by taking the needle from the right to the centre line.

Stitches alternate from left to right.

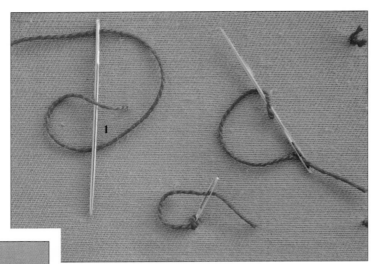

French knot

Bring the needle and thread out at 1 and hold the thread loop with your thumb. Slide the needle under the thread. Turn the needle in a clockwise direction and then take it down through the fabric near 1.

Long and short stitch

First row is worked from left to right. *Left-handed stitchers* work the first row right to left.

Row 1 is made up of alternating long and short stitches. The short stitch is about two-thirds the length of the long stitch.

In row 2 equal length stitches are made. Stitch down into the short stitches of the previous row, working from right to left (*left-handed stitchers* work left to right).

Needlewoven cup stitch

Make a base of three straight stitches in a triangular shape.

Work detached buttonhole stitch into the straight stitches without taking the needle into the fabric. On successive rows, work the buttonhole stitches into the loops of the previous rows of buttonhole stitch.

Ringed (raised) backstitch

Work a row of foundation stitches.

Slide the needle and thread under a foundation stitch, over the same stitch and back under the same stitch.

Move on to the next foundation stitch.

Needlewoven picot stitch

Following the numbers on the diagrams, bring thread out at 1 and down at 2, leaving a loop.

Pass a separate single strand of thread through the loop (yellow thread in the photograph).

Bring the thread out between 1 and 2 and take it under the holding thread. Hold the loop firmly with the separate holding thread while working the weaving.

Take the thread under the centre stitch.

Weave the thread under, over, under the three arms of the thread loop. Passing from right to left the threads are woven over, under, over. Passing from left to right to left the threads are woven under, over, under.

Continue weaving and pushing the threads towards the tip of the loop, until the loop is completely filled in.

Thread the holding loop down the centre back of the filled picot and take it into the fabric near 3. Pulling this thread tight can give a twisted shape to the petal. Refer to the bluebell photograph on page 58 for another illustration of working this stitch.

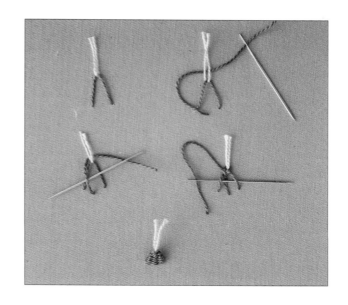

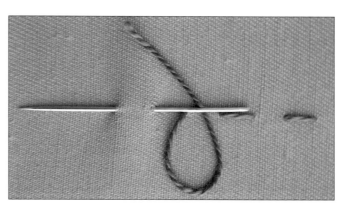

Needlewoven picot

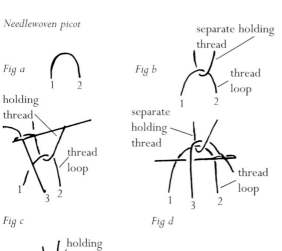

Running stitch

Worked from right to left.

Left-handed stitchers work from right to left.

Satin stitch

Worked from left to right. The stitches are worked close together.

Left-handed stitchers work from right to left.

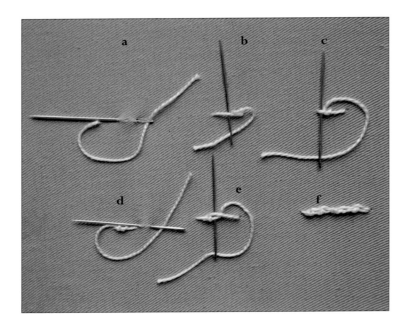

Second and succeeding stitches:

d Make another stem stitch.

e Pass the needle twice under the stitch just made and the previous stitch. Do not go through the fabric.

f Completed stitches

Left-handed stitchers work from right to left. I suggest placing the diagram in front of a mirror and working from the mirror.

First stitch

Fig a

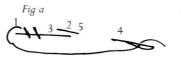

Fig b

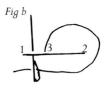

Fig c

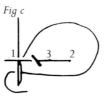

Portuguese stem stitch

Worked from left to right. I describe this stitch as a stem stitch with two wraps.

First stitch:

a Bring the needle up at 1 and down into the fabric at 2 to the right of 1. Bring the needle and thread out at 3, halfway between 1 and 2.

b Pass the needle and thread under the stitch just made; do not go into the fabric.

Second stitch

Fig a

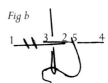

Fig b

Slip stitch

Used to attach slips to the embroidery.

Bring the needle and thread up at 1 in the background fabric only, under the applied shape.

Take the needle and thread down, picking up the folded edge of the applied shape, and into the background fabric under the applied shape.

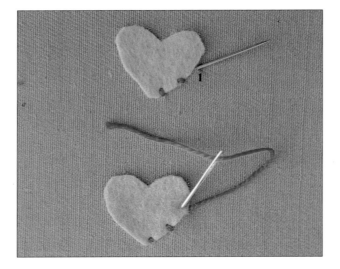

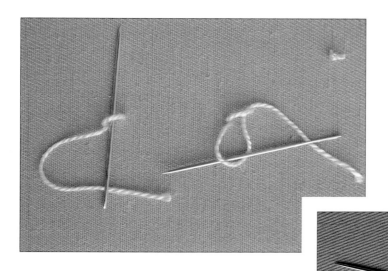

Smocker's knot

Pick up a small amount of fabric or threads.

Take the needle and thread through the loop.

Bring the needle and thread through the second loop and pull tight.

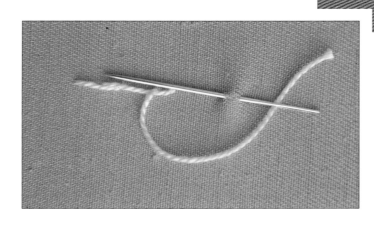

Stem stitch

Worked from left to right.

Bring the needle up at 1 and take it down at 2, to the right of 1 along the design line. Bring the needle up at 3 (between 1 and 2). The thread emerges from the top of the previous stitch.

Left-handed stitchers work from right to left.

Long stem stitch

Worked from left to right in the same way as stem stitch. The forward stitches are longer than normal stem stitch, up to 10 mm ($^3/_8$").

Pick up only a small amount of fabric when travelling from right to left.

Left-handed stitchers work from right to left.

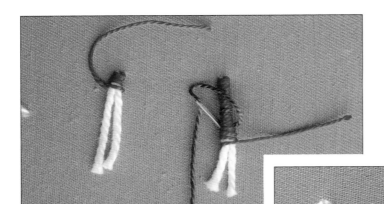

Wrapped threads are couched in position, using a separate thread the same as the winding thread. Couching stitches are about 3–5 mm ($^1/_8$") apart.

To join a new winding thread:

When the old thread is about 6 cm (2¼") long, take a new thread and anchor it firmly in one of the threads being wrapped close to where the last wrap is. Wrap over this join with the old winding thread.

Lay the old winding thread with the threads being wrapped, pick up the joined-in thread and continue winding the thread around the threads to be wrapped.

To vary the thickness of wrapped threads:

Always wrap from thick to thin, decreasing the thickness of the wrapped threads by dropping one and continuing to wrap the winding thread about the remaining threads.

Wrapped threads

Anchor threads must be fixed firmly in the fabric. Take the needle and thread in from the front, leaving a tail of thread the desired length. Bring the needle and thread to the front, close to where it went down, and leave a second tail of thread.

Anchor the winding thread firmly in the back and bring it to the front near the threads to be wrapped.

Hold the threads to be wrapped firmly in the left hand and wrap the winding thread around these threads in a clockwise direction.

Couch the wrapped thread in position; take the dropped thread to the back and anchor it in the backing fabric.

Part 2

THE FLOWERS

Chapter Three

WATTLE FLOWERS

WATTLE BELONGS TO the genus Acacia, which is the largest plant group in Australia, containing over 800 species. Golden wattle *(Acacia pycnantha)* is Australia's national flower. Wattles range in type from tall trees to small shrubs and are found in most areas of Australia. The flowers may be grouped into two types—round fluffy balls or cylindrical spikes, each of which is made up of a myriad tiny flowers grouped together. The colour of the flowers varies from light creamy yellow to deep orange yellow. Many of the species are sweet-scented.

Completed fluffy wattle project worked on a cream poly satin background

FLUFFY WATTLE

Requirements

20 cm (8") square background fabric
20 cm (8") square backing fabric
20 cm (8") square pelon
15 cm (6") hoop
strip of thin cardboard 1 cm x 8 cm ($^3/_8$" x 3"); cereal package thickness
B pencil
threads
    DMC Perle 8: 918 (red-brown)
    DMC Perle 5: 744, 725 (yellows)
    DMC Stranded Cotton: 744 (yellow) , 435 (tan),
    520 (green)
needles
    crewel 8 and 6
    chenille 22
    tapestry 24 or 26

Stitches

Running stitch, backstitch, whipping stitch, straight stitch, long stem stitch, French knot, smocker's knot

Fluffy wattle design

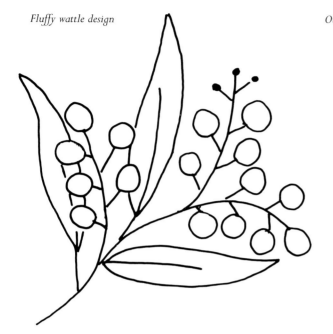

Outline for tracing onto calico

Flat embroidery for background fabric

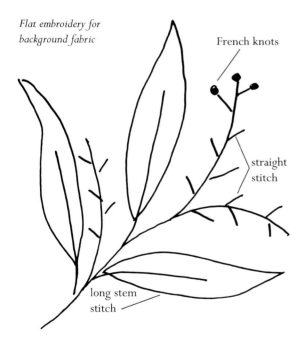

French knots

straight stitch

long stem stitch

Method

Trace the design outline onto the backing fabric, and place the backing fabric, pelon and background fabric in the hoop. Transfer the design outline to the front of the work with the method described on page 12, using a single strand of tan stranded cotton for the stem and a single strand of green stranded cotton for the leaves.

Leaf stalks

Work 1 row of backstitch with red-brown Perle 8 in a chenille 22 needle.

Using a single strand of tan stranded cotton in a tapestry needle, untidily whip the backstitch, making sure some of the red-brown thread shows through.

Main stems

Work two rows of backstitch along the stem line using chenille 22 needle and the red-brown Perle 8, making the stitches about 3 mm ($^1/_8$") long. The rows are worked close together and offset so the stitches do not stop and start at the same level on each row.

Anchor a strand of the red-brown Perle 8 and a single strand of tan stranded cotton at the base of the stem on the back of the work, and bring the threads to the front of the work. Lay the Perle 8 thread along the backstitched stem.

Thread the tan cotton into a tapestry needle and untidily whip together the two rows of backstitch and the thread of Perle 8. Some of the Perle thread should show between the wrapping threads.

The stalks of the wattle balls and flowerspikes are straight stitches, also worked in red-brown Perle 8.

Flat leaves

Using a crewel 8 needle and a single strand of green stranded cotton work a row of backstitch around the outside of the leaf shape.

To fill the leaf use 2 strands of green stranded cotton in a crewel 6 needle. Work a long stem stitch, starting from the outside of the leaf and working into the shape, following the photograph for guidance. Forward stitches should be about 10 mm ($^3/_8$") long. Keep the thread loop to the outside of the leaf. Make the stitches in each row stop and start at different levels to avoid creating horizontal lines across the leaf.

Work a row of backstitch down the centre to form the vein.

Buds

Using Perle 5 in either yellow (725 or 744) in a chenille 22 needle, work groups of 3 to 5 French knots on the ends of some of the wattle ball stalks.

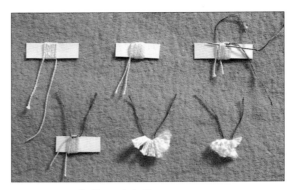

How to work a fluffy wattle ball

Thread a crewel 8 needle with 2 strands of green stranded cotton.

Wrap a Perle 5 yellow thread 7 times side by side across the width of the piece of cardboard. Wrap back over this row with a second row of thread.

Using the green cotton you have already threaded, and working from right to left, slide the needle and cotton under the first 4 yellow threads, leaving a tail of green cotton 8 cm (3") long. If you are left-handed work from left to right.

Slide the needle and green cotton under the same 4 yellow threads and anchor with a smocker's knot.

Work a row of backstitch across the wrapped threads, with each stitch picking up some already-stitched yellow threads and some unstitched yellow threads. Pull each stitch tight. At the end of row secure thread with a smocker's knot and leave an 8 cm (3") tail. The tails of cotton are used to anchor wattle balls to the embroidery.

Cut the wrapped threads along the unstitched side. Using the eye of a tapestry needle, separate the strands of the Perle thread, working from the stitching to the end of the thread. Place the wattle flowers in a small container until you are ready to attach them to your work.

Attaching the wattle balls

Before attaching the wattle flowers to the embroidery use sharp scissors to trim each fluffy ball to a maximum length of 6 mm (¼").

Thread one of the tails of green cotton into a chenille 22 needle, then take it through to the back of the embroidery and anchor it in the backing fabric. Repeat with the other tail of green cotton, taking it through to the back down the same hole as the first tail and anchoring the thread firmly.

After the wattle balls have been stitched in place gently re-fluff them with the eye end of a needle.

Steps in working the flat embroidery for fluffy wattle

Fluffy flowers

The 15 flowers are worked as detached balls which are attached to the work once all the flat embroidery is completed. Make roughly half in each of the two yellows.

CYLINDRICAL WATTLE FLOWERSPIKES

The cylindrical wattle flowerspikes are worked as slips (see page 12) and applied to the background fabric after the flat embroidery has been completed.

Requirements

20 cm (8") backing fabric
20 cm (8") square pelon
20 cm (8") square background fabric
10 and 15 cm (4" and 6") hoops
15 cm (6") square extra homespun or calico
2 pieces 12 cm (5") square Solvy (water-soluble fabric)
    for the detached leaves
12 cm (5") square organza for the detached leaves
threads
    DMC Perle 8: 918 (red-brown)
    DMC Stranded Cotton: 727 (yellow), 435 (tan),
    3346 or 3347 (green)

Cylindrical wattle flower spikes design

Design outline to be traced onto calico (backing fabric)

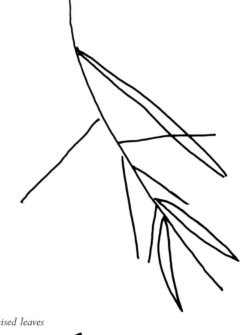

Flat embroidery for background fabric

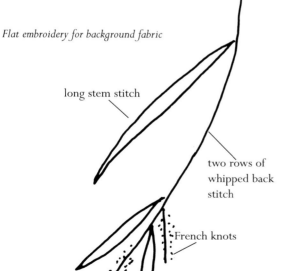

long stem stitch

two rows of whipped back stitch

French knots

Raised leaves

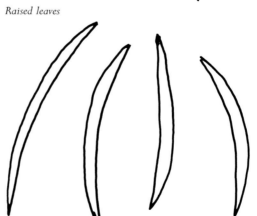

needles
    crewel 10 and 8
    chenille 22
    tapestry 24 or 26
    hand appliqué 12

Stitches

Running stitch, backstitch, whipping stitch, French knot, long stem stitch, slip stitch

Completed cylindrical wattle flowerspikes. The background is cream poly satin

Method

Trace the design outline onto the backing fabric and place the backing fabric, pelon and background fabric into the 15 cm (6") hoop as described on page 12. Transfer the design to the background fabric in running stitch,

using a single strand of tan stranded cotton for the stem and a single strand of green stranded cotton for the leaves.

Stem

The stem is worked in the same way as the main stem of the fluffy wattle (see page 27).

Buds

Randomly stitch French knots along the 2 bud stalks, using 2 strands of yellow stranded cotton in a crewel 8 needle.

Flat leaves

Outline the 3 leaf shapes with backstitch using a single strand of green stranded cotton. Continue with the single strand of green cotton to fill each leaf shape with long stem stitch, working from the outside of the leaf shape to the centre, and staggering the rows of stitching within the shape.

Cylindrical flowerspikes

On a piece of homespun fabric, using a B pencil, mark the lengths of the 6 flowerspikes on the fabric. Make sure the lines are drawn along the grain of the fabric. Place the fabric in a small hoop and keep it tight at all times.

Thread a crewel 6 needle with 2 strands of yellow stranded cotton and 2 strands of green stranded cotton and make 3 long straight stitches the length of the line and side by side. Work over these 3 stitches with French knots, randomly placed, with the remaining yellow and green thread.

Completely cover the straight stitches with more French knots worked with 3 or 4 strands of either of the two yellow stranded cottons, or a mixture of both shades.

When the slip embroidery is complete, use 2 strands of stranded cotton to work a row of running stitch around the shape 2 mm (³/₃₂") out from the embroidery. Paint outside the running stitch with a little PVA glue and allow to dry.

Cut out the shape along the glue line and pull up the running stitches. Use the excess thread to stitch the edges together.

Position the slip on the embroidery and slip stitch in place; place the first stitch at the tip of the flower spike and the second stitch at the base, then slip stitch along the sides.

You may want to add a few French knots along the sides after the flower spike has been stitched in position.

Detached leaves

The 4 detached leaves are worked on 2 layers of Solvy and a layer of organza. The organza holds the stitches together and the Solvy gives some stiffness to the leaf. Draw the leaf shapes on the organza with a pencil and place the 2 layers of Solvy and 1 layer of organza (on top) in a small hoop.

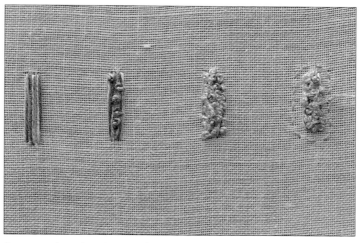

Steps in working the cylindrical flowerspikes

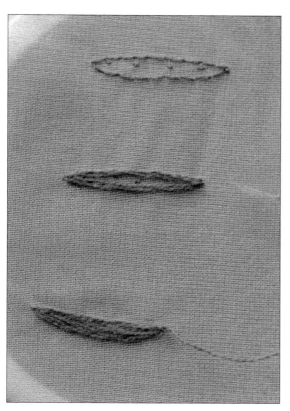

Working the detached leaves

> **TIP:** Keep moisture away from the Solvy while you are working with it, as it may dissolve.

Using a single strand of green stranded cotton in a crewel 10 needle and starting where the leaf joins the branch, work a row of backstitch around the leaf. Take the needle in from the front to begin the backstitch.

Fill in the shapes in the same way as the flat leaves, using long stem stitch, and working from the outside of the leaf to the centre. Leave a 10 cm (4") tail of thread at the leaf stalk end when embroidery is completed.

Remove the embroidery from the hoop and cut away the organza as close as possible to the stitching. Cut the Solvy 2 mm ($^3/_{32}$") from the stitching. Stick a fine needle through each shape and dunk each one in and out of water until the Solvy has disappeared from the edges, allowing some of the Solvy to remain within the shape. Pin out on a foam board to dry. When dry, trim away any fuzzy fibres and stitch in position, using the tail of thread left when you completed the stitching.

Chapter Four

GUM BLOSSOM AND GUMNUTS

Gum blossom and gumnuts embroidery worked on cream poly satin fabric

THE GUM TREE (*Eucalyptus* spp.) is widely recognised as Australian. Over 600 species of eucalypts are found in Australia, ranging from tall single-stemmed forest trees up to 60 m (200') in height to many-stemmed forms of mallee scrub less than 10 m (40') high. The flowers are very distinctive with no petals and masses of stamens, most often white or cream in colour. Brightly coloured red, pink, yellow and orange forms are also found.

Requirements

20 cm (8") square background fabric
20 cm (8") square pelon
20 cm (8") square backing fabric
10 and 15 cm (4" and 6") hoops
extra 15 cm (6") square washed calico or homespun
8 cm x 4 cm (3" x 2¼") brown felt
8 cm x 15 mm (3" x ½") thin cardboard (from a cereal packet)
2 nails 1.6 mm diameter
30 gauge green covered wire
cardboard circle, diameter 3 mm (¹/₈"); the cut-outs from a hole punch are ideal
PVA glue
threads
    DMC Stranded Cotton: 502 (light blue-green), 503 (blue-green), 839 (brown), 841 (light brown), 3787 (grey-brown), 435 (tan), 320 (black)
    DMC Soft Cotton no.4: 839 (brown)
    Cifonda Silk: 161 (yellow) or 115 (pink)
needles
    crewel 8 and 9
    chenille 20

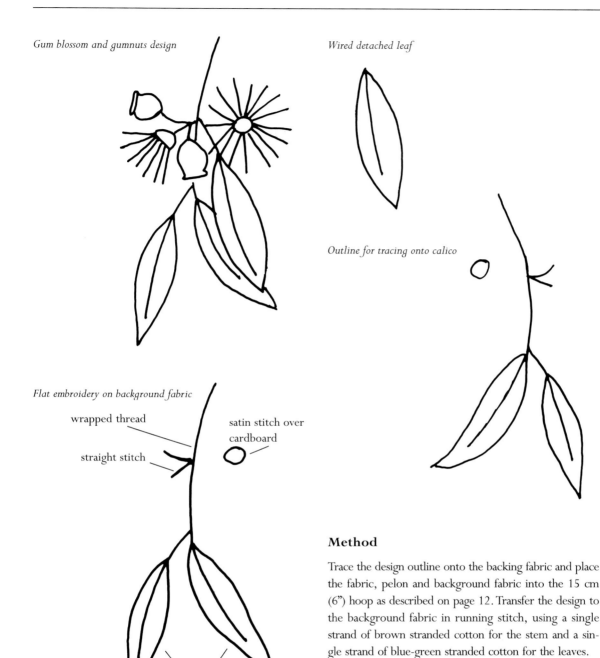

Gum blossom and gumnuts design

Wired detached leaf

Outline for tracing onto calico

Flat embroidery on background fabric

wrapped thread

satin stitch over cardboard

straight stitch

fishbone stitch leaves

hand appliqué 12
chenille, largest possible, or yarn darning needle

Stitches

Stitches

Running stitch, couching, backstitch, fishbone stitch, straight stitch, wrapped threads, satin stitch, cut turkey stitch, buttonhole stitch, stem stitch

Method

Trace the design outline onto the backing fabric and place the fabric, pelon and background fabric into the 15 cm (6") hoop as described on page 12. Transfer the design to the background fabric in running stitch, using a single strand of brown stranded cotton for the stem and a single strand of blue-green stranded cotton for the leaves.

Main stem

The wrapped threads for the stem are worked from the base of the stem to the leaves.

Thread 30 cm (12") brown soft cotton no.4 into a chenille needle. At the base of the stem take the thread in from the front, leaving a 15 cm (6") tail of thread. Bring the needle and thread through to the front again, close to where you took the needle down.

Anchor a single strand of light or mid brown stranded cotton on the back of the work and bring the thread through to the front, as close to the tails of thick thread as possible. Use the stranded cotton to firmly wrap the two thicker threads together.

Use a separate single strand of stranded thread (the same colour as the wrapping thread) to couch the wrapped threads into position along the stem line. Bring the couching needle out on the stem line over the wrapped thread and down into the same hole. The couching stitches should be about 3 mm ($^1/_8$") apart.

About 2 cm (¾") from where the stem splits, join in a second wrapping thread by anchoring another stranded thread to one of the threads being wrapped. Continue, wrapping all the threads with the first wrapping thread until the join is just covered.

At this point, separate the two thick tails of thread and wrap each one separately, couching them down to form the leaf stalks. Take the thick threads to the back about halfway along the leaves and anchor them.

Gumnut stems

Work straight stitches for the stems of the gumnuts, using 3 strands of the same thread you used as the wrapping thread for the main stems.

Flat leaves

Using a single strand of blue-green stranded cotton in a crewel 8 needle, work a row of backstitch around the 2 leaf shapes. With 2 strands of the blue-green stranded cotton in a crewel 8 needle fill each leaf shape with fishbone stitch. Use a longer thread than normal.

Fishbone stitch for gum leaves

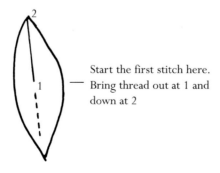

Start the first stitch here. Bring thread out at 1 and down at 2

Work straight stitches in a single strand of light or mid brown stranded cotton for the vein lines.

> **TIP:** To give the appearance of a gum leaf the first stitch of the fishbone stitch must come from halfway down the leaf vein. See diagram.

Gum blossom and gumnuts project showing the partially worked flat embroidery, with stems and one leaf worked in fishbone stitch. The other leaf is outlined with backstitch. Stalks coming from the main wrapped stem are worked in straight stitch

Detached leaf

For detailed instructions for detached embroidered wired shapes, see page 13.

Trace the leaf shape onto washed calico and place in a small hoop. Shape the wire. With a single strand of blue-green stranded cotton couch the wire around the leaf shape, beginning along the vein about 7–8 mm (¼") from the tip of the leaf, then working around the outside of the leaf.

Pad the shape inside the wire with straight stitches in 5 strands of blue-green stranded cotton. Fill the leaf shape with fishbone stitch, using 2 strands of blue-green stranded cotton in a crewel 8 needle. Take the thread through the fabric as close to the inside of the wire as you can. Do not cover the wire with the filling stitch.

Satin stitch over the wire using a single strand of blue-green stranded cotton, bringing the needle up in the embroidery and down on the outside of the wire.

Stitch in the veins using straight stitch and a single

strand of mid or light-brown stranded cotton.

Cut out the shape and put to one side, adding it to the embroidery after attaching the gumnuts.

Open gum blossom

This is worked on the background fabric after all the other flat embroidery has been completed.

Thread a crewel 8 needle with 1 strand of any green stranded cotton and anchor it to the fabric at the central point of the gum blossom. Holding the tiny disc of card on this spot, work a cross-stitch over it in the green thread to anchor it to the background fabric. Following the photograph, work satin stitch over the disc, stitching from one quarter to the opposite quarter. The stitches should cross in the centre.

Using 6 strands of Cifonda silk in your chosen colour, work two rows of cut turkey stitch around the covered disc of card, with the loops about 2 cm (¾") long. On the first row work the loops against the card with the flat stitches to the outside. Tie the loops together with a single thread. On the second row work the loops to the outside with the flat stitch against the flat stitch of the first row. Tie the loops together with a thread.

Side view gum blossom

This tassel is worked to a specific length because not all the loops of the tassel are cut.

Thread a single strand of green stranded cotton doubled into a crewel 8 needle.

Cut 50 cm (20") of Cifonda silk in your chosen colour and wrap it around a piece of card 15 mm (⁵⁄₈") wide about 13 times in a V shape.

Slide the needle and green thread under the threads forming the tip of the V and back through the loop in the green thread. Pull firmly. Slide the needle and thread under the threads again, in the opposite direction, and secure with a smocker's knot. Remove the tassel from the card, wrap a second strand of green thread around it 2 mm (³⁄₃₂") from the top to form the waist and knot securely. A second pair of hands to hold the tassel while you tie the thread is helpful.

Attach the tassel to the embroidery by threading the green thread at the top into a chenille needle, taking the thread to the back, anchoring it securely.

Thread the waist-tie threads into a chenille needle, take to the back of the work and secure. Cut some of the tassel loops, using the photograph as a guide.

Work green satin stitch to cover the top of the tassel.

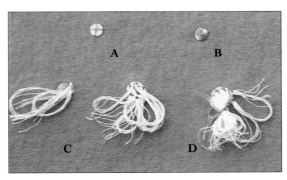

Stages in working the open gum blossom.
A Use two straight stitches in the form of a cross to anchor the disc of card to the fabric
B Use green thread to cover the card. Stitch from one quarter to the diagonally opposite quarter
C Work a row of cut turkey stitch around the covered card shape
D Tie the loops of the first row together.Work a second row of cut turkey stitch around the card shape

Trim the gum blossom at the end of the job, when all the other work has been completed. Before you do this, moisten the silk with a damp cotton bud, so it will lie flat.

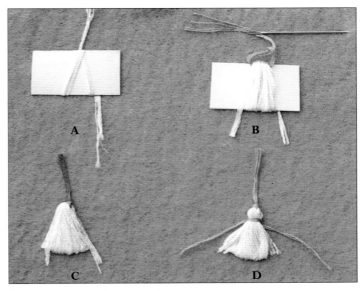

Stages in working a side view gum blossom.
A Wrap thread around the card in a V shape
B Slide needle and thread under the tip of V and through thread loop
C Slide tassel off the card
D Tie a thread at the waist of the tassel 2 mm (¹⁄₈") from the top of the tassel

Gumnuts

The gumnut is worked around a bead of felt and attached to the embroidery when the flat embroidery has been completed.

Pattern for gumnut felt bead

Cut a felt shape following the pattern. Wrap the narrow end of the felt piece around a nail, brush PVA glue onto the rest of strip and wrap it firmly around nail, keeping the edge straight. Allow to dry on the nail. The indented end of the felt roll is the stalk end of the gumnut.

Thread a tapestry 22 needle with 2 strands of grey-brown stranded cotton, 1 strand of mid brown or tan and 1 strand of light brown.

Take the threads through the centre of the hole from the stalk end, leaving a 6 cm (2½") tail, around the bead and through the hole again. Give the thread a tug, and repeat until the bead is completely covered. To finish, anchor the thread where you first entered the bead.

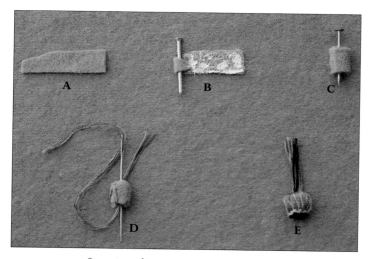

Stages in making a gumnut.
A Cut out the felt shape
B Wrap the narrow end of the felt around the nail and spread the remainder of the felt with glue
C Wrap the glued felt around the nail. Allow to dry
D Take threads through the centre and around the felt bead
E Completed gumnut

With 2 strands of black stranded cotton, go down through the centre and work a row of open buttonhole stitch around the rim of the gumnut, with the loops of the buttonhole stitch to the outside.

With 2 strands of the lightest colour you have used, work a row of stem stitch against the ends of the buttonhole stitches (see photograph).

Squash the gumnut into shape between your fingers.

Half gumnut

The half gumnut is worked in the same way as the full gumnut, only covering two-thirds of the felt bead with thread.

When the stitching is completed, cut away small Vs from the visible felt to remove the excess, and squash the gumnut in your fingers to make it flatter.

Attaching the gumnuts

Thread all the tails of thread into a large chenille needle and take through to the back of the embroidery, leaving 1–2 mm (about ¹/₁₆") on the front of the work to form the stalk.

Thread a crewel 8 needle with 1 strand of the colour used for the stem and anchor the tails of thread firmly on the back, take this single strand to the front of the work and wrap the stalk. Slip stitch the sides of the half gumnut to the fabric.

Attaching the detached wired leaf

Take the wire from the detached leaf through to the back of the embroidery (following the instructions on pages 13–14). Stitch the wire down on the back of your work with a single strand of thread matching the background fabric, positioning the wire so that it lies in the same direction as the leaf. Bring the thread to the front and wrap the wire stalk, anchoring the thread at the base of the leaf.

Cutting the open gum blossom

Remove the thread keeping the loops of cut turkey stitch together and cut the loops with sharp scissors, leaving threads 10 mm (³/₈") long. Carefully moisten the cut threads with a damp cotton bud and use a tapestry needle to stroke them into position. Trim the individual threads again to achieve the effect you want. Blow gently on the threads to dry and fluff them.

Chapter Five

FLANNEL FLOWER

THE FLANNEL FLOWER (*Actinotus helianthi*) is an annual herb, flowering in spring and summer, that can grow 1 m (40") high. It is found along the coast and lower ranges in New South Wales and southern Queensland.

The leaves and stems are grey-green and furry. The flowerheads are white to cream, tipped with green, and consist of clusters of florets surrounded by 7–18 petal-like bracts which are covered with fine hairs.

Requirements

20 cm (8") square backing fabric
20 cm (8") square pelon
20 cm (8") square background fabric
10 cm and 15 cm (4" and 6") hoops
20 cm (8") square firm iron-on interfacing
9 cm (3½") square doctor flannel or cream wool fabric
Gladbake paper or appliqué mat
60 cm (24") fine wire (34 gauge beading wire or 34 gauge paper/thread covered wire)
1 cm x 6 cm (³/₈" x 2¼") thin cardboard
Matisse Acrylic Folk Art paint in Antique Green and
    Antique White
PVA craft glue
flat brush no.4
white tile or saucer
threads
    DMC Stranded Cotton: 3053 (grey-green), ecru or
    712 (cream), 435 (tan)
    DMC Soft Cotton no.4: grey-green or grey
    Appleton's Crewel Wool: 342 (grey-green)
needles
    crewel 8
    chenille 20
    large yarn darner or chenille
    hand appliqué 12

Completed flannel flower project worked on pale green silk

Flannel flower design

Detached petals

Flat embroidery

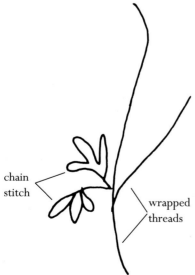

chain
stitch

wrapped
threads

Design outline for tracing

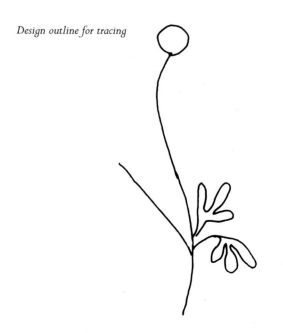

Stitches

Running stitch, couching stitch, backstitch, chain stitch, whipped chain stitch

Method

Trace the design outline onto the backing fabric, and place backing fabric, pelon and background fabric into the 15 cm (6") hoop as described on page 12. Transfer the design to the background fabric in running stitch, using a single strand of grey-green stranded cotton.

Stem

Wrapped threads are used for the stem.

Thread 30 cm (12") soft cotton into a chenille 20 needle. Take the needle in from the front at the base of the stem, leaving a 15 cm (6") tail of thread. Bring the needle and thread through to the front close by, leaving another tail of thread.

Using a crewel 8 needle, anchor a strand of the grey-green wool in the background fabric, bring to the front as close to the base of the tails of thread as possible, and wrap the 2 tails of thread together for 10 mm (³/₈"). Join in a second wrapping thread of grey-green wool, anchoring the new thread in one of the soft cotton tails as close to the wrapped thread as possible.

Continue wrapping with the first wrapping thread, covering the join, until you reach the split in the stem.

Again using the grey-green wool in a crewel 8 needle, couch the wrapped stem in place, working from the base of the stem upwards.

> **TIP:** Bring the needle out on the stem line, around the wrapped threads and down in the same hole, every 4 mm (³/₁₆").

When you reach the split in the stem, separate the two strands of soft cotton and wrap each one separately to become the flower stem and the bud stem. Couch the two wrapped stems in position.

Take the threads through to the back and end off securely.

Leaves

Thread a crewel 8 needle with the grey-green wool and work chain stitch around the leaf shape. Continue in chain stitch, filling in the shape.

The leaf stalk is formed by whipping two rows of chain stitch together.

Flowers

These are worked as separate wired shapes and attached after the stems, leaves and bud are completed.

Partially worked flat embroidery for the flannel flower, showing the wrapped and couched stem, worked leaves and bud in position

Trace the 11 flower petal shapes and 3 bud petal shapes onto the non-shiny side of the iron-on interfacing (these are the reverse of the finished petal shapes). Place the doctor flannel on the shiny side of the interfacing. Cover the fabrics with Gladbake paper or appliqué mat and bond together. Remove the paper and place fabrics in the 10 cm (4") hoop with the interfacing to the top and the doctor flannel on the underside of the hoop.

Cut a 5 cm (2") length of 34 gauge beading wire and fold in half. Using a single strand of cream stranded cotton in a hand appliqué needle, anchor the thread at the base of the leaf shape and work small backstitches along the vein line, finishing near the tip of the petal.

Lay the wire along the vein line, with the folded end towards the petal tip. Bring the needle up in the fold in the wire and satin stitch over the doubled wire down to the base of the petal. Hold the needle and thread at right angles as they enter and leave the fabric. When you bring the needle and thread up from under the hoop give the thread a small tug to firmly anchor the wire.

> **TIP:** To finish, use the method for finishing eyelet holes. Work plain satin stitch to the last 2 stitches. Leave the last 2 satin stitches as loops. Bring the needle up close to the first loop and slide needle and thread through both loops. Pull the second loop tight to lock the thread under the first loop. Now pull on the tail to anchor the thread under the second loop. Cut the thread.

 Fig a Last two stitches worked leaving loops

 Fig b Bring the thread out above the fist loop and take the needle and thread through the loops.

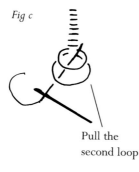 Fig c

Pull the second loop

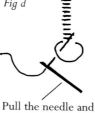 Fig d

Pull the needle and thread. Cut the thread off close to the satin stitch

Work each flower petal in the same way, using a new thread for each one, as stitching over wire abrades and weakens the thread.

Stages in attaching the wire along the vein line of the flannel flower petals. The wire has been coloured and coloured stitches used to emphasise the stitching line

Bud petals

With a single strand of cream stranded cotton in a crewel 8 needle work a row of stem stitch down the vein lines of the 3 bud petals.

Cut out all the bud and petal shapes when you are ready to colour the edges and attach them to your work.

Colouring the petal shapes

Number the shapes on the back with a pencil (I work around the flower in a clockwise direction) and cut out each petal. Do not cut the wire tail.

On a tile or saucer mix a little dot of Antique Green paint into Antique White to make a delicate pale green. Mix in an equal quantity of white PVA craft glue, adding a little water to make it runny. Push or apply the paint mixture down the side of each petal and brush paint over the tip. (I find it easiest to hold the petal wrong side up and gently push the side of the brush against the edge of the petal.)

Attaching the petals

Buds Position the side petals first, catching them down in 2 or 3 places along the outside edge with a slip stitch, using 1 strand of cream stranded cotton.

Position the centre petal on top of the side petals and slip stitch it down at the base and the middle of each side. Leave the tip free.

Flower Working around the circle for the centre of the flower, and starting with petal no.1, take the wire from the petal through to the back, following the instructions on pages 13–14.

Stitch the wire in position under the petal's position with a single strand of cream stranded cotton, anchoring each petal in turn. Use tweezers to tease the petals into their final position.

Flower centre

The centre of the flannel flower is a fluffy wattle ball made using 2 strands of crewel wool and 4 strands of cream stranded cotton (see page 28). Fluff and trim the ball and attach it in the centre of the flower.

Chapter Six

WARATAH

THE WARATAH *(Telopea speciosissima)* is the state emblem of New South Wales. A shrub 3–4 m (10'–14'), it grows in the sandy soils of the coast and tablelands of New South Wales, its bright showy flowers appearing in spring *(telopea* means 'seen from afar'). The leathery leaves are a long oblong shape with serrated edges; the red flowerheads consist of numerous tubules surrounded by red bracts.

The waratah is worked on cream poly satin and has embroidered leaves

Requirements

20 cm (8") backing fabric
20 cm (8") square pelon
20 cm (8") square background fabric
10 cm and 15 cm (4" and 6") hoops
15 cm (6") square washed calico or quilter's muslin
15 cm x 30 cm (6" x 12") red poly lining fabric (a little lighter than DMC Stranded Cotton 814)
30 gauge pink and green covered wire
34 gauge beading wire or covered wire
20 cm (8") square olive-green fabric for bonded leaves
15 cm (6") square Vliesofix
threads
    DMC Stranded Cotton: 936 and 937 (olive-green), 3053 (green), 814 and 816 (garnet red), 329 (pink-red)
    DMC Perle 5: 420 (tan), 816 (garnet red)
needles
    crewel 8 and 6
    hand appliqué 12
    chenille 20
    large chenille or yarn darning needle

Stitches

Running stitch, backstitch, satin stitch, straight stitch, bullion stitch, couching stitch

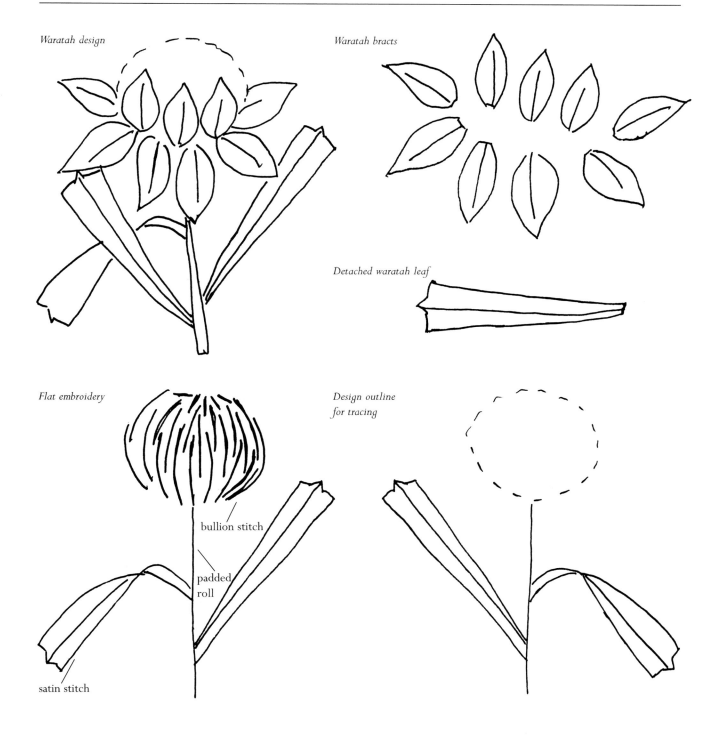

Waratah design

Waratah bracts

Detached waratah leaf

Flat embroidery

bullion stitch

padded roll

satin stitch

Design outline for tracing

Method

The waratah can be worked with either fabric or embroidered leaves (or both).

Trace the design outline onto the backing fabric and place backing fabric, pelon and background fabric in the 15 cm (6") hoop as described on page 12. Transfer the design to the background fabric with running stitch, using a single strand of olive-green cotton for the embroidered leaves and the stem and a single strand of light garnet red to outline the flowerhead.

If you wish to use bonded fabric leaves work running stitch in olive-green cotton along the leaf vein line.

Stem

This is a padded roll.

Cut 10 lengths tan Perle 5 twice the length of the stem + 5 cm (2").

Fold the threads in half and anchor them, through the fold, at the top of the stem line with another length of the same thread, using a crewel 6 needle.

Twist the threads together and couch in position along the stem line, making a stitch every 5–7 mm (about ¼"). Bring the needle out on the stem line over the threads and down in the same place.

At the end of the stem wrap the couching thread firmly around the stem 3–5 times and end the thread in the wrapped threads. Cut the wrapped threads as close to the wrapping as possible.

Take another length of tan Perle 5 and satin stitch or whip over the couched roll of threads. Bring the needle out under the roll and sloping away from it, and take it in under the roll.

Embroidered flat leaves

Outline the leaf shape and central vein with back or split stitch using a single strand of olive-green stranded cotton.

Fill the outlined shape with satin stitch, using 2 strands of olive-green cotton in a crewel 8 needle. Bring the thread out on the vein line and take it down to the outside of the outlining stitches.

> **TIP:** Before beginning to fill in with satin stitch, put in a few straight stitches, using a single strand of thread, as guide lines for the stitch direction.

The leaf veins are straight stitches in 1 strand of light yellow-green cotton; the central vein is 2 strands of light green cotton, couched down with a single strand of the same thread.

A single row of backstitch can be worked around the edge of the leaf if you wish, using light yellow-green cotton. This adds to the illusion of depth.

Embroidered raised leaf

This is a detached embroidered wired shape (see pages 12–13 for detailed instructions).

Partially worked flat embroidery for the waratah. The leaves in this instance are bonded fabric held in place with couched threads

Trace the leaf shape onto washed calico or homespun and place fabric in a small hoop.

Use a single strand of olive-green cotton to couch 30 gauge covered wire around the shape. Begin at the base of the leaf, working around the leaf shape to end back where you started. There is no wire down the central vein of the leaf.

Fill inside the wired shape with satin stitch, using 2 strands of olive-green cotton. Work from the mid-vein to the outer edge, taking the stitches as close to the wire as you can.

Using a single strand of light yellow-green cotton work the side veins with long straight stitches.

Work tiny satin stitch over the wire with a single strand of olive-green cotton in a hand appliqué 12 needle, bringing needle up in the embroidery and down outside wire.

Cut out the leaves and attach them to the work after you have worked the waratah flowerhead.

A few small stitches may be needed between the leaf and background fabric to hold the leaf in place.

Flat fabric leaves

Trace the leaf shapes onto the Vliesofix. Lay Gladbake on the ironing board, then the Vliesofix, with the tracing against the Gladbake. Lay the fabric on top of the Vliesofix. Cover with a second piece of Gladbake and use a dry iron to bond the fabric.

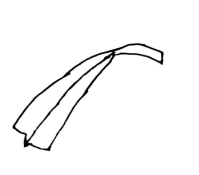
Bonded fabric flat leaves for the waratah project

Cut around the leaf shape. Position it on the background fabric so that the vein line is along the running-stitched vein line. Cover with Gladbake and use the iron to bond the shape in position.

Lay 2 strands of light olive-green stranded cotton around the leaf and couch in position with a single strand of the same thread. The central vein is 2 strands of light olive-green cotton couched in position and the other leaf veins are straight stitches worked with a single strand of stranded cotton.

Raised fabric leaves

Trace the detached leaf shape onto olive-green fabric. Bond to a second piece of fabric so the traced line is visible.

Place the bonded fabric in a hoop. Couch the wire down the central vein and around the edge of the leaf with a single strand of light olive-green stranded cotton. Leave a tail of wire at the stalk end of the leaf. Stitch over the central vein wire with satin stitch using a single strand of light olive-green stranded cotton.

Cover the wire around the shape with buttonhole stitch worked with light olive-green cotton. The loops of the buttonhole stitch are on the outside of the shape. Remove from the hoop and cut out the shape.

Waratah flowerhead

The waratah flowerhead is worked in four layers. Colour the area behind the bullion stitches with a crimson watercolour pencil before you start stitching.

First layer: The background bullion stitches, worked in a rather loose messy fashion.

Work the bullion stitch using garnet red Perle 5 in a chenille 20 needle, leaving gaps between the bullions at the base of the flowerhead. Work 4 rows of bullions as shown in the first diagram on page 46.

Second layer: Wrapped threads. Use the second diagram on page 46 as a guide to position the two rows.

With 2 lengths of garnet red Perle 5 cotton in a chenille needle, and starting near the top of the flowerhead, take the needle in from the front and make a small stitch, bringing the needle out as close as possible to where the thread went in, leaving 4 tails 12 mm (4½") long.

Now secure 3 strands of dark garnet red stranded cotton at the same point and bring these threads to the front.

Firmly wrap the Perle threads with the stranded cotton, working a little further than the flat length required so the wrapped thread will stand above the bullions. Secure all threads on the back.

Make 2 rows of 6 wrapped threads, using about 20 wraps for the first row and 25 wraps for the second row.

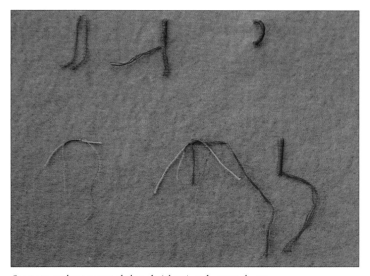
Stages in making wrapped threads (above) and wrapped wire fingers (below) for the waratah flowerhead

Third layer: Wrapped wires—twenty detached wrapped wire fingers (see page 46).

Cut 20 x 6 cm (2¼") lengths of pink cotton covered 30 gauge wire.

Wrap 1 strand of pink stranded cotton around the centre of the wire for 10 mm (³/₈"). Fold the wire in half.

Knot 3 strands garnet red stranded cotton on one side of the folded wire, leaving a tail of thread 12 cm (5") long, and use the long tail of red and pink threads to firmly wrap the doubled wire. Wrap only the length required for each finger. Knot the thread around the wire when the desired length is reached, usually somewhere between 22–27 wraps, or approximately 2 cm (¾").

To attach a wrapped finger, trim the wire and pink thread as close as possible to the wrapping thread, position the finger on the flowerhead and anchor it with the wrapping threads, taking them to the back of the work, one group of three threads at a time.

Bring a wrapping thread through to the front again if you need to make some small stitches over the wire finger to secure it in place.

Fourth layer: The wired bracts, which are bonded, wired and glued shapes.

Trace the bract outlines onto a piece of red poly lining fabric. These outlines are the reverse of the finished petal shapes.

Bond the poly fabric to a second piece of the same fabric, with the traced shapes on the outside (see page 15), and position in a 10 cm (4") hoop with the traced shapes facing up.

Anchor a single strand of dark garnet red stranded cotton at the base of the vein line, finishing near the tip of the bract.

Cut an 8 cm (3") piece of 34 gauge beading wire for each bract and fold in half. Bring the thread out in the fold of the wire and couch the doubled wire along the vein line with a satin stitch.

> **TIP:** To end the stitching use the method for finishing eyelets. Leave the last 2 stitches as small loops. Bring the needle up close to first loop and slide needle and thread through both loops. Pull the second loop tight to lock thread under first loop, then pull the tail to anchor thread under the second loop. Cut the thread (see page 40).

When you have stitched the wire along all the vein lines, leave the work in the hoop and paint both sides of the fabric, in and around each bract, with a mixture of 75% white PVA glue, 25% water.

Leave to dry. Cut out each shape, place a pin at the base and position on the main embroidery. Stitch the bracts in place following the instructions on pages 13–14, and adjust their positions with tweezers.

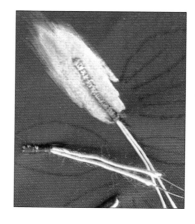

Wire is stitched down the centre vein of the bract and the fabric shape painted with glue and water

Placement of bullion stitches
Number of bullion wraps
Row 1: 4, 4, 5, 4, 4, worked left to right
Row 2: 9, 7, 7, 7, 7, 7, 7, 9
Row 3: 12, 11, 11, 11, 11, 11, 12
Row 4: 12, 12, 12, 12, 12, 12, 12,

Wrapped thread placement guide
Starting at the top of the flower head:
Work 2 rows of wrapped threads
Row 1: 5 wrapped threads x 13 mm (⅝") long
Row 2: 6 wrapped threads x 15 mm (¾") long

Wrapping a wire finger

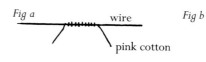

Fig a   wire

pink cotton

Fig b   red stranded cotton

wire

Fig c

*C*hapter Seven

BOTTLEBRUSH

BOTTLEBRUSHES (Family Myrtaceae, genus *Callistemon*) are evergreen shrubs and trees, weeping or upright in form. The brush-like flowers are made up of masses of bright coloured conspicuous stamens that grow on the tips of the branches. The new leaves grow from the brush tips and the spent flowers become woody seed capsules. Bottlebrushes may be red, pink, cream or purplish mauve.

Requirements

20 cm (8") square backing fabric
20 cm (8") square pelon
20 cm (8") square background fabric
15 cm (6") hoop
10 cm (4") double-sided 12 mm (½") satin ribbon in green to match DMC Flower Thread 937
PVA craft glue
flat paint brush no.4
threads
   DMC Stranded Cotton: 3787 (grey-brown), 937 (green), 435 (tan), 888 (red), 321 (crimson), 744 (yellow)
   DMC Flower Thread: 937 (green) or 2 strands of Stranded Cotton 937
needles
   tapestry needles 26 and 22
   chenille needle 22
   crewel needles 8 and 5

Stitches

Running stitch, backstitch, whipped chain stitch, cup stitch, needlewoven picot, tufting

Completed bottlebrush project worked as a centre for a paperweight. The background fabric is cream poly satin

Method

Trace the design outline onto the backing fabric and place backing fabric, pelon and background fabric into the 15 cm (6") hoop as described on page 12. Transfer the design to the background fabric in running stitch, using a single strand of grey-brown stranded cotton for the stem and olive-green for the leaves.

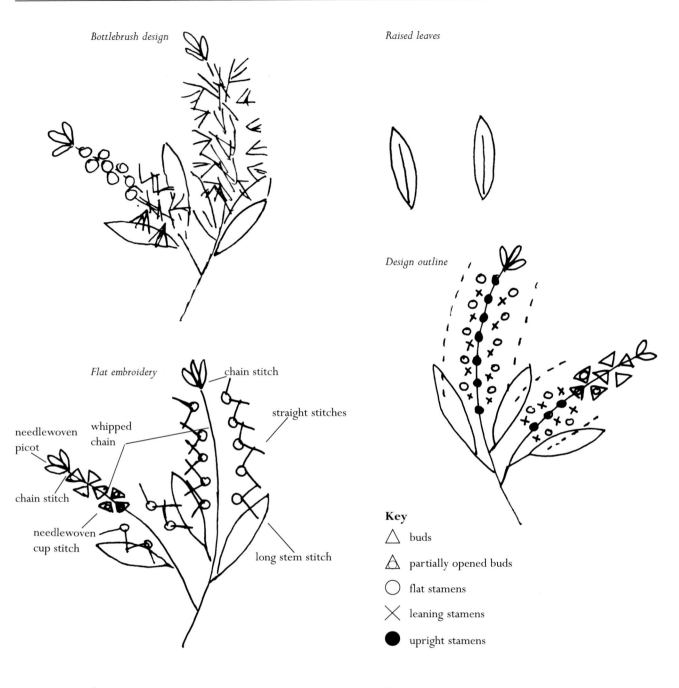

Bottlebrush design

Raised leaves

Design outline

Flat embroidery

chain stitch

straight stitches

needlewoven picot

whipped chain

chain stitch

needlewoven cup stitch

long stem stitch

Key

△ buds

⊿ partially opened buds

○ flat stamens

✕ leaning stamens

● upright stamens

Stem

With 4 strands of grey-brown stranded cotton in a crewel 5 needle, work a chain stitch down each stem, starting at the tips.

Whip the chain stitch with 4 strands of stranded cotton (1 strand each tan and grey-brown and 2 strands brown) in a tapestry 22 needle. The whipping stitches do not go into the fabric but pass between the fabric and chain stitches.

Leaves

Outline the 3 leaf shapes with backstitch using a single strand of green stranded cotton in a crewel 8 needle. To fill the leaf use 2 strands of green stranded cotton is a crewel 8 needle. Work long stem stitch, starting from the outside of the leaf and working into the shape. Keep the thread loop to the outside of the leaf.

Work the leaf stalks in stem stitch in 1 strand of the same green.

Flower tips

Work 3 long chain stitches on top of each other at the main stem tip, using a single strand of green stranded cotton. This gives you a fat, filled chain stitch.

Work 2 slightly shorter filled chain stitches in the same way, one each side of the first one.

For the partially opened brush, work just 2 filled chain stitches in the same way.

The bud at the tip is a needlewoven picot worked in 2 strands of tan stranded cotton (see page 21 for instructions).

Buds

Indicated by the 4 triangles at the top of the secondary stem.

The unopened buds are worked in needlewoven cup stitch using green flower thread or 2 strands of green stranded cotton (see page 20 for instructions).

Partially opened buds

Indicated by the last 3 triangles on the secondary stem.

Work green needlewoven cup stitch as above until the first row of detached buttonhole stitch has been completed. Thread a chenille 22 needle with 3 strands red, 3 strands crimson and 1 strand yellow stranded cotton; bring the needle out in the centre of the bud and take it to the back close by, leaving a loop of thread 1–2 mm high. Anchor the threads in the backing fabric.

Finish working the needlewoven cup stitch in green around the loop.

Open bottlebrush flowers

A combination of flat stitches and tufted stitches, following the design outline.

Flat stitches Represented as open circles on the design outline.

Thread a chenille 20 needle with 4 strands red, 4 strands crimson and 1 strand yellow stranded cotton. Bring the threads to the front in the circle. Anchor a second needle (crewel 8), threaded with green flower thread or 2 strands of green stranded cotton, in the back and bring to the front as close as possible to the red threads.

Wrap the green thread firmly around the red and yellow threads 4 times; take the green thread to the back and park the needle out of the way.

Fan out the yellow and red threads and take them to the back, 2 threads at a time, 6 mm (¼") from where they emerged.

Regroup the yellow and red threads, thread into the chenille needle and repeat this step along the length of the stem. (I've got to admit this step is a bit fiddly. Try not to twist the red and yellow threads with the green threads.)

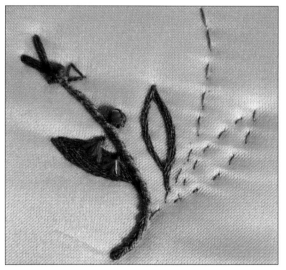

Bottlebrush project as a work in progress. The stem tip is two chain stitches worked over each other. Also shown is a needlewoven cup stitch bud, a partly worked bud and a partially open bud. One leaf is shown completed with flat stamens embroidered over it; the other leaf is being filled with long stem stitch from the outside of the leaf to the centre.

Tufted stamens Here again it is very easy to get the red and yellow threads twisted with the green thread.

The lines of leaning and upright stamens (**x** and ● on the diagram) are worked the same way.

Thread the chenille 22 needle with 4 strands red, 4 strands crimson and 1 strand yellow stranded cotton.

Work the **x** stitches first, then the ● stitches. Anchor the threads in the back, bring to the front where indicated by the **x** or the ● on the design outline, and take them to the back, leaving a loop of thread about 15 mm (⁵⁄₈") long.

Anchor a second needle (crewel 8) threaded with green flower thread in the back and bring the needle to the front as close as possible to the loop of red and yellow threads.

Wrap this thread firmly around the loop of red and yellow threads 3 times, then take it to the back through the loop (✗ stamens).

To make the tufts lean, hold the wrapped loop of thread in the direction you want it to lie and take the needle and green threads down through the wrapped section of the loop (● stamens).

For upright tufts, hold the loops vertical and take the needle and green thread down through the centre of the wrapped loop.

When all the tufts are made, slide a needle into each individual loop and trim to the required length with sharp scissors.

Raised leaves

Mark the 2 leaf shapes onto the double-sided green satin ribbon with a pencil.

Using 1 strand of green stranded cotton and starting at the tip of the leaf, work a row of backstitch down the vein of the leaf. Leave a tail of thread at the end to attach the leaf to the embroidery.

Paint both sides of the ribbon with a solution of 75% glue, 25% water, covering the leaf shape and the area around it. When the glue is dry and all the other embroidery has been completed, cut out the shape and attach it to the work, using the tail of thread.

Manipulate the leaves into position with tweezers.

Chapter Eight

TEA-TREE

THE TEA-TREE (*Leptospermum* spp.) is a common shrub up to 2 m (6") high. Most species flower abundantly, making a great show, appearing from spring through to late autumn. The flowers are open with five petals, in colour white or cream through to pinks and reds.

The name tea-tree arose because Captain Cook's sailors are believed to have used the leaves as a substitute for tea.

Requirements

20 cm (8") square backing fabric
20 cm (8") square pelon
20 cm (8") square background fabric
20 cm (8") square firm non-iron interfacing (Vilene)
15 cm (6") hoop
34 gauge beading wire
PVA glue
needles
    crewel 7 and 10
    chenille 20
    hand appliqué 12
    yarn darner
threads
    DMC Stranded Cotton: 3787 (grey-brown), 895 (bright green), 225 (pale pink), 223 (pink), 3721 (dark pink), 3346 (light green)
    DMC Soft Cotton no.4 in a light colour

Stitches

Running backstitch, Portuguese stem stitch, long stem stitch, satin stitch, chain stitch

The tea-tree project, worked on a cream poly satin background, features wired embroidered petals

Method

Trace the design onto the backing fabric and place backing fabric, pelon and background fabric into the 15 cm (6") hoop as described on page 12. Transfer the design to the background fabric with running stitch, using a single strand of grey-brown cotton for the stem, a single strand of bright green for the leaves and a single strand of pale pink for the bud and the centres of the flowers.

Stem

Work the small stem first, then the main stem.

For the small stem use 2 strands of grey-brown cotton in a crewel 8 needle to work Portuguese stem stitch along the stem line.

The main stem is Portuguese stem stitch worked in 4 strands of grey-brown stranded cotton.

Work from base to tip of the stem, making the stitches longer as you work up the stem to vary the thickness.

Leaves

Leaves of the tea-tree may be very thin and pointed or broader with pointed tips.

Work the thin pointed leaves as three straight stitches using a single strand of bright green thread in a crewel 8 needle. Work a central stitch first, no more than 5 mm ($^3/_{16}$") long, then work a shorter stitch on either side, coming out at the same place at the base of the leaf. The leaves alternate from side to side along the stem.

The broader leaves are worked using a single strand of bright green stranded cotton. Start by working a backstitch around the outside of the leaf shape. Fill the leaf shape with a long stem stitch, using 2 strands of bright green cotton in a crewel 8 needle and working from the outside of the leaf shape to the inside.

Buds

Outline the bud shape in backstitch using a single strand of pale pink cotton. Using soft cotton no.4 work 3 padding stitches as shown in Fig. 1a. Cover the padding stitches with satin stitch, using 1 strand of pale pink stranded cotton in a crewel 9 needle. The satin stitch is worked from the stem to the tip.

The 2 bud sepals are formed by working satin stitch diagonally over the bud stitches, using a single strand of bright green thread Fig. 1d.

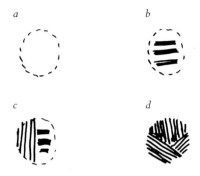

Fig. 1 Working the tea-tree bud

Flowers

The flowers, 5 spreading petals surrounding a central disc, can be worked in two ways—either as detached wired shapes or as needlelace shapes. (Not everyone enjoys working needlelace.)

A: Wired detached petals

The individual petal shapes are small and can be worked on firm non-iron-on Vilene, which doesn't leave little fraying bits when the shape is cut out.

Draw the individual petal shapes onto the Vilene, leaving a space of 15 mm (½") around each petal.

Using a single strand of pink stranded cotton, work a row of chain stitch around each shape. Fill the shapes with satin stitch. (I work 3 directional stitches as guides, then fill the rest of the shape.) Bring the thread up inside the chain stitch and down at the base and sides of the petal (Fig. 2).

Cut a 5 cm (2") length of 34 gauge beading wire and place it around the shape on top of the chain stitch,

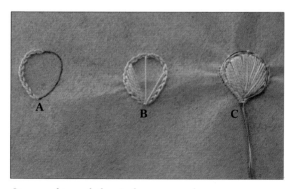

Stages used to work the wired tea-tree petal.
A Chain stitch around the edge of the shape
B Place in 3 directional straight stitches; fill shape with chain stitch
C Wire is satin stitched in place on top of the chain stitch

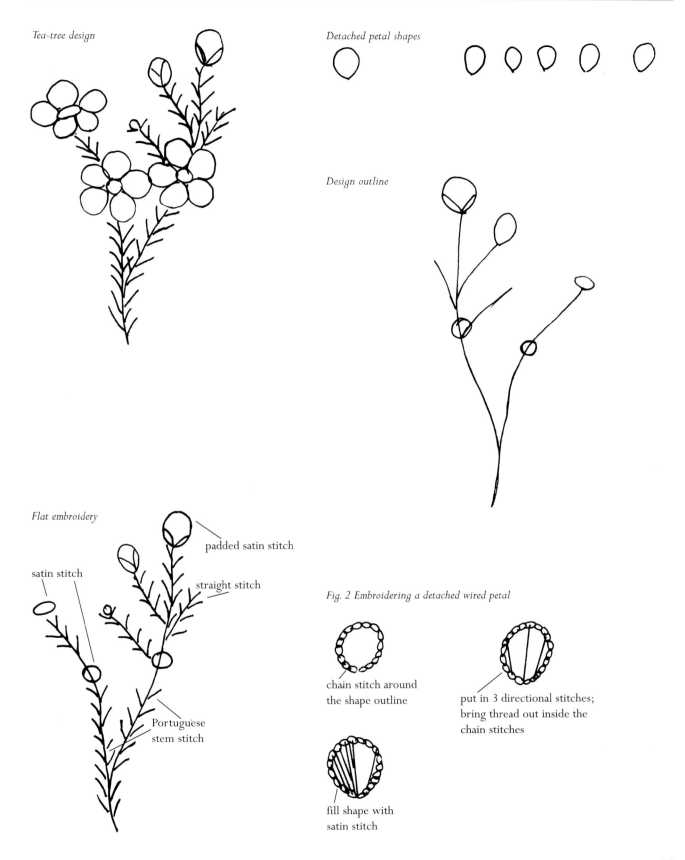

Tea-tree design

Detached petal shapes

Design outline

Flat embroidery

padded satin stitch

satin stitch

straight stitch

Portuguese
stem stitch

Fig. 2 Embroidering a detached wired petal

chain stitch around
the shape outline

put in 3 directional stitches;
bring thread out inside the
chain stitches

fill shape with
satin stitch

Fig. 3 Placement of buttonhole stitch for needlelace petals

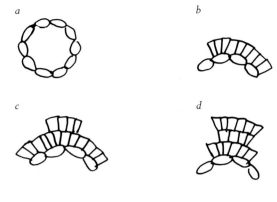

a   b

c   d

e

Tea-tree flowers with needlelace petals. This is a close-up of the tea-tree flowers featured in the wildflower wreath (page 92). To soften the contrast between the fabric and the stitchery, the background fabric has been printed with maidenhair fern leaves dipped in olive-green folk art paint mixed with textile medium.

using the pink thread to satin stitch it in position. Bring the thread up in the embroidery and down on the outside of the chain stitching. Cut out the 5 petal shapes and attach them to the completed flat embroidery at equal distances.

> **TIP:** See pages 14–15: Marking equal divisions around a circle.

Flatten the petals down against the work and fill the centres of the flowers with satin stitch, using a single strand of dark pink stranded cotton.

For a particularly realistic touch, work a row of cut turkey stitch around the centre, using 2 strands of bright green cotton, to represent the stamens. Make 10 mm ($^3/_8$") loops and paint them with PVA glue, cutting the loops to length when the glue is dry.

B: Needlelace petals

Needlelace tea-tree petals are also worked on firm non-iron-on Vilene. (I advise practising first, working petals around a circle 10 mm ($^3/_8$") in diameter with Perle 5 thread.)

For the actual project, draw a 5 mm ($^3/_{16}$") circle on the Vilene and mark 5 equal divisions around it. (I usually trace around the little piece cut out by a hole punch.) Following Fig. 3a, work 2 chain stitches in each division of the circle (10 chain stitches), with a single strand of dark pink stranded cotton

Each petal is worked separately. Thread the dark pink thread into a tapestry needle 24 or 26 and work 3 buttonhole stitches in each chain stitch (30 buttonhole stitches). Stitch into the chain stitch only, not into the fabric. End the thread in the flower centre (Fig. 3b).

Thread the tapestry needle with pink thread and anchor the thread in the flower centre. Work a buttonhole stitch into each of 4 stitches from the previous row (Fig. 3c). Do not stitch into the fabric; these stitches are detached. Turn the work and work buttonhole stitch back along the row, increasing by 1 stitch at the beginning and end of each row. Work 4 more rows in the same way (Fig. 3d).

To shape the top of the petal work 3 rows, decreasing 1 stitch at each end (Fig. 3e). Run the thread down the back of the petal, miss 1 buttonhole stitch in the foundation row, and start a new petal.

When all the petals have been worked, push them away from the fabric and cut away the Vilene as close as possible to the stitching.

Attach the flowers to the flat embroidery by working satin stitch across the centre, using a single strand of dark pink thread.

The stamens can be represented by cut turkey stitch, using 2 strands of bright green stranded cotton. Make the loops 10 mm ($^3/_8$") long. Paint the finished loops with PVA glue and trim to length when dry.

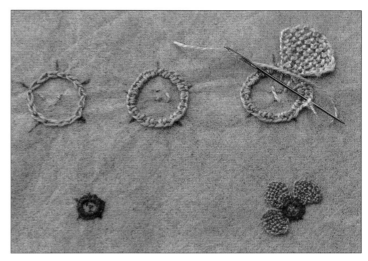

Stages in working the needlelace tea-tree petals. The top row shows a practice petal, made with Perle 5 thread around a 10 mm ($^3/_8$") circle; the bottom row shows a half-finished flower made with stranded cotton around a 5 mm ($^3/_{16}$") circle

Chapter Nine

NATIVE BLUEBELLS

THE BLUEBELL (*Wahlenbergia stricta*) is the floral emblem of the Australian Capital Territory. It is closely related to the bluebells of the northern hemisphere. Bluebells are slender herbaceous plants with blue bell-like flowers. They grow between 15–45 cm (6"–18") tall with pale green leaves at the base and blue flowers carried on slender stems. Each stem may carry many flowers.

Completed bluebell project worked on cream poly satin

The flowers can vary in colour from pale blue to an intense blue-purple. Bluebells are found in open country in the eastern States and Tasmania, and flower from late spring through summer into autumn.

Requirements

20 cm (8") square backing fabric
20 cm (8") square pelon
20 cm (8") square background fabric
15 cm (6") hoop
threads
    DMC Stranded Cotton: 918 (red-brown), 3347 (green), 435 (tan), 793 (medium cornflower blue), white
    DMC Perle 8: 918 (red-brown)
    Cifonda Silk: 174 (yellow)
needles
    crewel 5 and 8
    tapestry 24 or 22

Stitches

Running stem stitch, whipped stem stitch, satin stitch, straight stitch, French knot, needlewoven picot

Method

Trace the design outline onto the backing fabric and place backing fabric, pelon and background fabric into the 15 cm (6") hoop as described on page 12. Transfer the design to the background fabric with running stitch, using a single strand of green stranded cotton for the stems and a single strand of cornflower blue stranded cotton for the buds.

Australian bluebell design

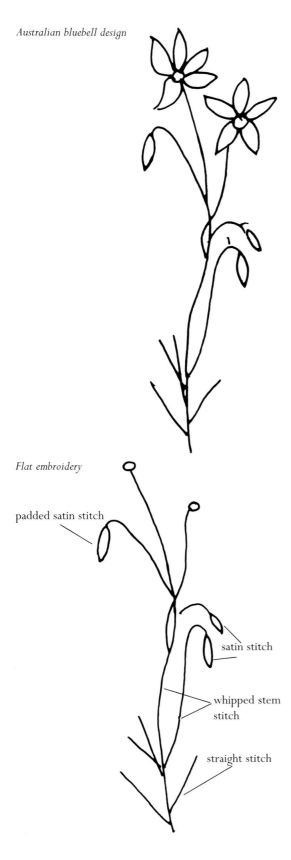

Design outline

Flat embroidery

padded satin stitch

satin stitch

whipped stem
stitch

straight stitch

Stems

Work a row of stem stitch along the 3 bud stems, using 2 strands of red-brown stranded cotton in a crewel 8 needle. Whip along the stem stitch with 1 strand of green stranded cotton in a tapestry 22 needle. Allow some of the red-brown thread to show through the whipping thread.

At the top of each stem, where the bud joins the stem, whip the red-brown stem stitch with 2 strands of tan stranded cotton for about 10 mm ($^3/_8$").

Work along the main stem line and the other flower stem with stem stitch, using red-brown Perle 8 in a crewel 5 needle. Whip the stem stitch with 2 strands of green stranded cotton threaded in a tapestry needle, allowing some of the red-brown thread to show through.

Leaves

Each leaf is worked in long straight stitches the length of the leaf. Using 2 strands of green stranded cotton in a crewel 8 needle work two long stitches side by side. Start the stitches very close together at the base of the leaf; give the tip of the leaf a little shape by making one stitch slightly longer than the other.

Partly opened buds

The 2 buds are worked in padded satin stitch. Bud shapes can be drawn onto the fabric with pencil or the shape can be outlined in backstitch using a single strand of blue stranded cotton.

Thread 3 strands of blue stranded cotton in a crewel 5 needle and work padding stitches across the bud shape. Work satin stitch over the padding stitches, from bud tip to the stem, with a single strand of blue stranded cotton.

Make the bud sepals in fly or straight stitch, using 2 strands of green thread.

Unopened bud

This bud is worked using 2 strands of tan stranded thread in a crewel 8 needle; work a series of 6 straight stitches over each other, bringing the needle in and out the same hole and alternating the thread from one side of the stitch to the other as you work.

Work a single green straight stitch over the tan stitches.

Flowers

Each flower is made up of 5 needlewoven picots worked around a circle, using 3 strands of blue stranded cotton in a crewel 5 needle. Keep the strands of thread together by rubbing them gently over a beeswax block.

Draw a circle 3 mm ($^1/_8$") in diameter on the fabric. (For this I usually trace inside the hole cut by a hold punch in a piece of card.) Mark 5 equal divisions around the circle with a pencil.

Anchor the 3 strands of blue cotton firmly in the centre of the circle. Working clockwise, bring the needle up on one of the division marks and then take it down on the next division mark, leaving a loop of thread 6–8 mm (about ¼") long. Take a single strand of blue stranded cotton through the loop and hold it firm as you work the needlewoven picot. See page 21 for detailed instructions.

Fill the middle of the flower with French knots worked in 2 strands of white stranded cotton, adding a single French knot worked in yellow silk in the centre.

Steps in working a needlewoven picot. Work five petals around the circle

Chapter Ten

MAIDENHAIR FERN

MAIDENHAIR FERNS (*Adiantum* spp.) have fan-shaped fronds with pale green fan-shaped leaflets.

Requirements

20 cm (8") square backing fabric
20 cm (8") square pelon
20 cm (8") square background fabric
10 cm and 15 cm (4" and 6") hoops
20 cm (8") square Solvy
fine pins
small polyfoam board
threads
    DMC Stranded Cotton: 3346 (pale green), 3347
    (green), 938 (dark brown)
needles
    crewel 8
    tapestry 24

Stitches

Running stitch, whipped stem stitch, detached chain stitch

Method

Trace the design outline onto the backing fabric and place backing fabric, pelon and background fabric in a hoop as described on page 12. Transfer the design outline to the background fabric with running stitch, using a single strand of dark brown stranded cotton for the stem. The leaflets are not marked on the fabric, but should be placed to make an attractive pattern. Make sure some of the leaves are stitched over each other.

Maidenhair fern project

Maidenhair fern design

Flat embroidery

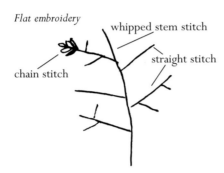

whipped stem stitch

straight stitch

chain stitch

Design outline

Flat leaflet

a Work central chain stitch first

b Work a chain stitch either side

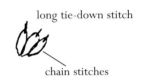

long tie-down stitch

chain stitches

Stem

c Fill between chain stitches

Stem

Using 2 strands of dark brown stranded cotton in a crewel 8 needle, work a row of stem stitch along the stem line. Whip the stem stitch with 2 strands of dark brown stranded cotton in a tapestry needle.

Leaf stalks

Each leaf stalk is a straight long stitch, worked from the stem to the stalk tip in a single strand of the dark brown or green cotton in a crewel 8 needle.

Flat leaflets

Position the leaflets to make a pleasing background pattern. With a single strand of green thread in a crewel 8 needle, work each leaflet as 5 detached chain stitches of about the same length, coming out at the same place at the base of the leaf and fanning out at the top. Make longer than usual tie-down stitches. Fill between these long stitches with smaller chain stitches fanning out from the base (see diagram above).

Raised leaflets

I suggest working 5–7 raised leaflets.

Place two layers of Solvy in the 10 cm (4") hoop. To start, using a single strand of light green stranded cotton in a crewel 8 needle, take the thread in from the front, leaving a tail of cotton 10 cm (4") long.

Bring the needle and thread up 2 mm ($^1/_{16}$") from where you went in, deliberately splitting the thread tail as you come up.

Work the detached leaflets in the same way as the flat leaflets, but without the longer tie-down stitches. As you finish each leaflet, bring the thread out at the base where you started. This provides two tails of thread which are used to stitch the leaflet in position.

Cut out the individual leaflets leaving 2 mm ($^1/_{16}$") of Solvy around the embroidery. Place a pin through the base of leaflet and dunk it quickly into cold water, repeating the dunking if necessary. The Solvy should disappear from around the embroidery but don't overdo it—some Solvy should remain inside the embroidery to provide stiffness. Pin out on a piece of foam board to dry.

Attaching the raised shapes

Using a crewel needle, take the tails of thread to the back of the embroidery separately and anchor them in the backing fabric.

Chapter Eleven

BUTTERFLIES AND OTHER BEASTIES

BUTTERFLY

A BUTTERFLY has a head, thorax, abdomen, six legs, hooked antennae, hind wings and fore wings. The abdomen is half the total body length and the thorax is one-third the remaining length. The wings and legs are attached to the thorax.

The Wanderer butterfly described in this section appears in the Waratah and Insects embroidery shown on page 75 and the front cover.

This beautiful sewing box worked by Jennifer Kime features butterflies on the lid, with caterpillars, a spider and its web inside.

Requirements

20 cm (8") square silk screen fabric 10txxx (or 2 layers silk organza bonded together)

10 cm (4") hoop

34 gauge beading wire or 34 gauge covered wire

threads

Cifonda Silk in the appropriate butterfly colours; Wanderer butterfly colours are white, black and orange 135A

DMC Stranded Cotton: 3371 (black-brown), 320 (black)

chenille thread in dark brown (optional)

DMC Soft Cotton no.4 in a dark colour

black petite glass beads

needles

crewel 10 and 8

hand appliqué 12

chenille 20

straw (milliner's) needle

Stitches

Satin stitch, wrapped threads, chain stitch, whipped chain stitch, straight stitch, long stem stitch, cut turkey stitch, French knot.

Detail of worked butterfly. This butterfly is from the Waratah with Insects project. The instructions given are for working this butterfly.

Method

Head

Using a single strand of black stranded cotton in a crewel 10 needle, satin stitch the head shape. Working across the head from eye to eye. Stitch two petite glass beads on to form the eyes.

Thorax

The thorax is worked after the wings are attached, either as three rows of cut turkey stitch up the body line, using 6 strands of dark brown cotton, or as a single straight stitch in chenille thread.

Abdomen

The abdomen is made using wrapped threads.

Starting at the thorax end, and using dark soft cotton no.4 in a chenille needle, take the thread in from the front and leave a 5 cm (2") tail of thread. Bring the needle and thread up close to where it went down and leave another tail of thread. Now, using a crewel 10 needle, anchor a single strand of black-brown stranded cotton in the backing fabric and bring to the front as close as possible to where the tails of thread come out of the fabric.

Wrap the thick threads for the required length with the single strand of cotton, then take the two thick threads to the back. The wrapped threads should stand clear of the fabric.

Add some extra windings of wrapping thread to the centre region of the abdomen to fatten it, then take the thread to the back and use it to anchor the thick threads on the back of the work.

Detached wings

Trace the wing shapes onto the silk screen or bonded organza fabric using an HB pencil and place the fabric in a hoop.

Using a single strand of black stranded cotton in a crewel 10 needle, work a row of chain stitch around the outside of the wing shapes.

Using black silk thread, work a whipped chain stitch along the inner veins of the wings. The diagram shows a method of working the whipped chain so that it will be continuous.

Satin stitch the fine wire around the outside of the wing, using a single strand of black stranded cotton in a hand appliqué 12 needle.

Wing shapes for Wanderer butterfly

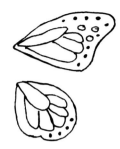

Placement of legs and foundation stitches for the caterpillar

foundation body
stitches

head padding stitches

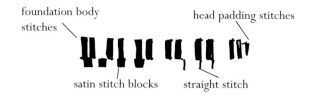

satin stitch blocks   straight stitch

Feelers

back stitch tip

straight stitch

Chain stitch outlines

whipped chain
stitch

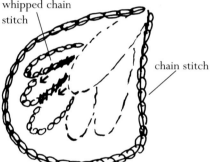

chain stitch

← direction of whipping stitches

Spider web

a Couch the spokes

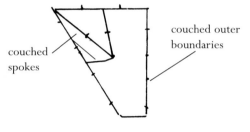

couched
spokes

couched outer
boundaries

b Fill the web

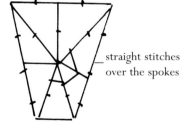

straight stitches
over the spokes

c Working the straight stitch

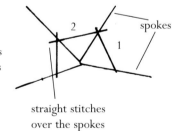

2   spokes

1

straight stitches
over the spokes

whip over the
outer chain
stitches

Spider legs are chain stitches

To fill the centre of the wing, work the small areas of colour first, e.g. the white dots, in satin stitch. Fill in the larger areas of colour using a combination of satin stitch and long stem stitch where longer stitches are required. Hold the embroidery up to the light to make sure there are no gaps between stitches.

Carefully cut the wings out as close to the stitching as possible.

Attach the wings at the thorax area, the hind wings first, then the fore wings. Now work the flat embroidery for the thorax area.

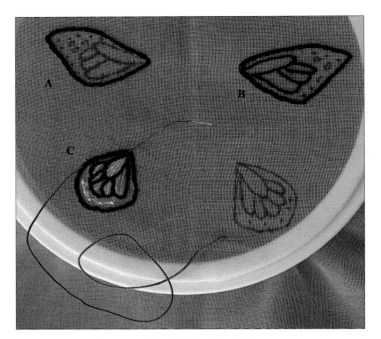

Stages in working Wanderer butterfly's wings.
A Chain stitch around the outer shape
B Centre veins are stitched with whipped chain stitch
C The segments are filled with satin stitch in the appropriate colours. Wire is satin stitched in place over the chain stitch before the inner black satin stitch is worked.

Antennae

Use a single strand of black silk thread to work a straight stitch from the head with a French knot at the tip, or wrap a single strand of black silk thread around the centre of a piece of fine wire for 4 mm ($^1/_8$"), bend the wire at the wrapped section and continue wrapping with the silk for the length required.

CATERPILLAR

This is a smooth bodied caterpillar.

Requirements

threads
    DMC Soft Cotton no.4 in a light colour for the body
    black stranded silk thread
    DMC Stranded Cotton: white, 946 (orange), 320 (black)

black petite glass bead
needles
    chenille 22
    crewel 10 and 8
    tapestry 24

Stitches

Straight stitch, ringed backstitch, satin stitch, backstitch

Detail of worked caterpillar

Method

Legs

Following the diagram, work the front legs as straight stitches and the back legs as satin stitch blocks, using a single strand of black stranded cotton in a crewel 10 needle.

Head and body

Using soft cotton thread in a chenille needle work a foundation row of straight stitches as shown in the diagram. The stitches are worked loosely so needle and thread can be passed under them.

Using a single strand of soft cotton in your chosen colour in a tapestry 24 needle, work rows of ringed backstitch along the foundation straight stitches for the body. Bring the needle and thread out from under the three head stitches and work along the body, working always from the head to the end of the caterpillar. The foundation stitches should be well covered.

Cover the foundation stitches for the head with satin stitch, using 2 strands of black silk thread in a crewel 8 needle. Stitch a petite glass bead in place for the eye.

Vertical stripes along the caterpillar's body are straight stitches worked with a single strand of black silk thread.

Feelers

The feelers can be flat or raised and curved. Flat feelers are embroidered in long straight stitches with a small backstitch at the tip; use a single strand of black silk thread.

Raised feelers are begun with a knot in the end of a single strand of black stranded cotton. Paint the knot and the cotton for the length of the feeler with PVA glue. When the glue is dry stitch the feeler in place and trim the cotton close to the knot at the tip.

SPIDER AND WEB

Spiders weave their webs in a logical order, first putting in place the outer boundaries or guys of the web, then the spokes, and finally joining the spokes in a circular manner. An embroidered web is worked in the same way.

Requirements

threads
    machine metallic thread (e.g. Madeira machine thread Astro-1, silver or gold)
    clear machine thread
    black stranded silk or cotton thread
black petite glass bead
black glass bead

Stitches

Straight stitch, couching, chain stitch

TIP: When using metallic threads work with short lengths only. If the thread has many filaments, glue the cut ends together with PVA glue. This makes threading the needle easier.

Method

Web

Couch the outer boundaries in position, working with metallic thread and couching down with clear or metallic thread. Working from the centre of the web, couch the metallic thread spokes in position. Using a single metallic thread in a crewel needle and working from the centre of the web to the outside, fill in the web using straight stitches that go over the spokes, as shown in the diagram.

Detail of worked spider and web from the wildflower wreath project on page 92. The embroidery is worked on cream poly satin which has been painted. The web is metallic machine thread

Spider

Real spiders have eight legs, head, body and abdomen. For these projects, however, a spider is worked with only six legs, using two beads to represent the body and head.

Legs, body and head

Using a single strand of black silk thread or stranded cotton in a crewel 10 needle, work each leg as 2 chain stitches with a longer tie-down stitch at the end. Work 6 legs from a central point.

Use a glass bead for the body and a petite glass bead for the head, positioned with the rounded side, not the hole, facing up.

The lid of the sewing box on page 61

Part 3

PROJECTS WITH MIXED WILDFLOWERS

Chapter Twelve

WILDFLOWER POSY I

Requirements

30 cm (12") square backing fabric

30 cm (12") square pelon

30 cm (12") square background fabric

10 cm and 25 cm (4" and 10") hoops

15 cm (6") square firm interfacing (not the iron-on type)

15 cm (6") square Solvy

15 cm (6") square poly organza

8 cm (3") square doctor flannel or cream wool fabric

15 cm square (6") firm iron-on interfacing

small piece brown felt

60 cm (24") 34 gauge beading wire or very fine silk covered wire (diameter 0.012") for the tea-tree flowers

20 cm (8") 30 gauge paper covered wire for the gum leaf

60 cm (24") 34 gauge beading wire or fine silk covered wire (diameter 0.01") for the flannel flower

1 cm x 8 cm ($^3/_8$" x 3") cardboard

1.5 cm x 8 cm ($^5/_8$" x 3") cardboard

3 mm ($^1/_8$") diameter disc thin cardboard (centre from a hole punch)

PVA glue

soft sheet nail dia. 1.6 mm

threads

    DMC Stranded Cotton: 938 (dark brown), 3347 (light yellow-green), 3346 (yellow-green), 435 (tan), 3787 (taupe), 895 (bright green), 224 (light pink), 223 (pink), 3721 (dark pink), 502 (dark blue-green), 503 (blue-green), 712 (cream) or ecru, 839 (brown), 841 (beige)

    Cifonda Silk: 115 (pink)

    DMC Perle 5: 744 and 727 (yellows)

    DMC Perle 8: 918 (red-brown)

    DMC Soft Cotton no.4: grey or light brown

    Appleton's Crewel Wool: 342 (grey-green)

needles

    crewel 6, 8 and 10

    chenille 22

    tapestry 24

    hand appliqué 12

Stitches

Running stitch, whipped stem stitch, backstitch, Portuguese stem stitch, long stem stitch, chain stitch, satin stitch, cut turkey stitch, wrapped threads, whipping

Method

Transfer the design outline onto the backing fabric and place backing fabric, pelon and background fabric in the 25 cm (10") hoop as described on page 12. Transfer the design to the front in running stitch using a single strand of stranded cotton in the following colours:

maidenhair fern stem—dark brown

wattle:

    stem—tan;

    leaves—light yellow-green

tea-tree:

    stem—taupe;

    leaves—bright green;

    bud—pink

gum:

    stem—taupe;

    leaves—blue-green

flannel flower stem—taupe

Completed wildflower posy sampler piece featuring maidenhair fern, tea-tree blossom, fluffy wattle, gum blossom, gumnuts and flannel flower, worked on a black silk background

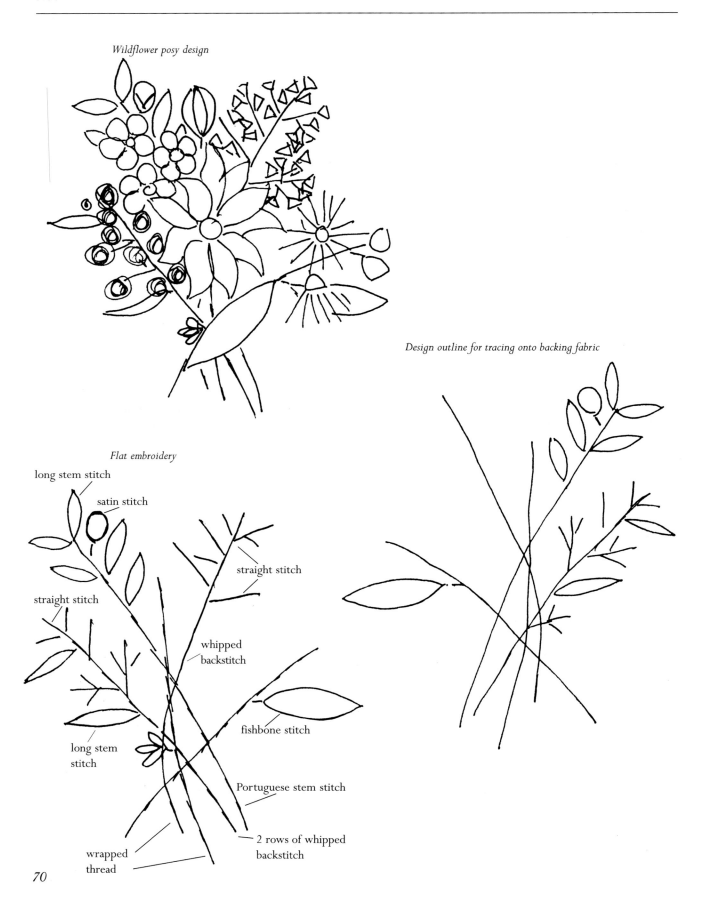

Wildflower posy design

Design outline for tracing onto backing fabric

Flat embroidery

long stem stitch

satin stitch

straight stitch

straight stitch

whipped backstitch

long stem stitch

fishbone stitch

Portuguese stem stitch

wrapped thread

2 rows of whipped backstitch

FLAT EMBROIDERY

For detailed instructions refer to the appropriate page for the native flower you wish to work. For the best result, stitch the flat embroidery in the order given.

Maidenhair fern

Backstitch along the stem line using 2 strands of dark brown stranded cotton. Whip the backstitch with 2 strands of the same thread.

Leaf stalks are long straight stitches worked in a single strand of dark brown or yellow-green stranded cotton.

Work the fern leaflets in detached chain stitch using a single strand of yellow-green stranded cotton.

Fluffy wattle

Work two rows of backstitch along the stem line in red-brown Perle 8. Lay another thread of red-brown Perle 8 on top of the backstitch and whip this thread and the two rows of backstitch with a single strand of tan stranded cotton. Some of the red-brown thread should show through the whipping thread.

Flower stems are straight stitches worked in red-brown Perle 8.

Work the buds in French knots using a single strand of yellow Perle 8.

Tea-tree

Work the stem line in Portuguese stem stitch using 4 strands of taupe stranded cotton.

Using a single strand of bright green stranded cotton, work a row of backstitch around each leaf shape and fill the leaf with long stem stitch.

The bud is a padded stitched shape, outlined in backstitch with a single strand of pink stranded cotton. The padding is provided by 3 or 4 straight stitches across the bud shape, inside the backstitching, worked in soft cotton. Work satin stitch over the padding stitches with 2 strands of pink stranded cotton. Work from the stem to the tip of the bud.

Cover the base of the bud with bright green straight stitches to represent the leaves covering the bud.

Flower centres are a circle 2 mm ($^{3}/_{32}$") in diameter. Using a single strand of dark pink stranded cotton outline the circle with backstitch and fill it with satin stitch or French knots.

Gum leaf and stem

The gum stem is wrapped threads, begun with 3 strands of soft cotton no.4 as the foundation. Wrap these 3 threads with a single strand of mid or light brown stranded cotton, working up from the base to the point where the gum leaf joins the stem. At this point take a second strand of thread the same colour as the wrapping cotton and couch the stem in place. Bring the needle and thread out on the stem line, over the thread and down in the same place.

Remove one of the thick threads, taking it to the back in the centre of the leaf, and continue wrapping and couching the remaining two threads to the end of the stem. Take the threads to the back and fasten off.

Outline the flat leaf using a single strand of blue-green cotton. Fill the leaf shape with fishbone stitch in 2 strands of blue-green cotton. Use a single strand of the stem colour and straight stitches to work the vein lines within the leaf.

Open gum blossom

The flower centre is a 3 mm ($^{1}/_{8}$") disc of cardboard covered with satin stitch in a single strand of any of the green stranded cottons. The stamens around the centre are worked in cut turkey stitch using the pink silk thread.

Work the first row so that the loops are over the centre disc and the flat stitches are to the outside. Work the second row with the loops to the outside and the flat stitches against the flat stitches of the first row.

Flannel flower

The stem of the flannel flower is wrapped threads. Use 2 lengths of soft cotton no.4 as the foundation threads and wrap them with a single thread of grey-green crewel wool. Couch the stem in place with the grey-green wool.

RAISED EMBROIDERY

Maidenhair fern Make 10 detached leaves (see pages 59–60).

Wattle Make 12 fluffy wattle balls and 2 detached leaves (see page 28).

Tea-tree Make 15 individual flower petals (see pages 52–53).

Gum blossom, gumnuts and leaf Make 1 side view gum blossom tassel, 1 gumnut and 1 half gumnut, and 1 detached gum leaf (see pages 34–36).

Wildflower posy showing the completed flat embroidery surrounded by the raised pieces ready to assemble

Flannel flower Make 3 bud petals, 10 flower petals, and 1 fluffy wattle ball in flannel flower colours (see pages 28 and 38–40).

Attach the raised pieces to the completed flat embroidery in the following order.

Maidenhair fern Leaving the leaflets on their pins, place them in position. When you are satisfied with the appearance stitch them in place.

Wattle Trim the threads of the wattle balls evenly, to a maximum length of 4 mm (¼"); and then refluff the flowers. Stitch them in position along the wattle stem.

Detached raised pieces

Teatree

petal shape

flower shape

Flannel flower petals

bud shape

Wattle leaves

Gum leaf

You may find you do not need to use all the wattle balls you have made. Position the two detached wattle leaves amongst the wattle balls.

Tea-tree Mark 5 equally spaced pencil dots around each flower centre (see pages 14–15) and attach a petal at each point. You may wish to work a row of cut turkey stitch around each flower centre using a single strand of green stranded cotton. Paint the stitches with glue and trim when the glue is dried.

Gumnuts Thread all the tails of thread at the top of the gumnut into a large needle, take the threads to the back of the work and anchor them, leaving 2 mm ($^1/_8$") thread exposed at the front of the work. Wrap these exposed threads at the base of the gumnut to the stem, with a single strand of cotton matching the stem thread colour. A few slip stitches may be needed to keep the nuts in position.

Side view gum blossom Take the threads at the top of the tassel to the back and anchor them, then take the threads at the waist of the tassel to the back and anchor them. Cover the top of the tassel with green satin stitch, and cut some of the tassel loops.

Flannel flower I find this trick helpful—take a tracing of the flannel flower on tracing paper, push a pin through the centre and use it to find the best position for the flower on the embroidery. Mark this point with pencil. Stitch the flannel flower bud in place—first the right petal, then the left, then the central petal, all attached at the base and centre. The petal tip should be free. Attach the flannel flower petals around the pencil mark. Fill the centre of the flower, either with French knots in grey-green wool or with a wattle ball made with grey-green wool and cream thread.

Detached gum leaf Position the leaf, take the wire to the back and anchor it. Any visible wire can be wrapped with a single strand of cotton in a colour to match the stem.

Open gum blossom Moisten the threads with a damp cotton bud and trim them to size. Blow on the threads to dry them and trim again if necessary.

The wildflower posy is now ready for mounting.

Chapter Thirteen

WARATAH WITH INSECTS

THIS DESIGN features a waratah, Wanderer butterfly, caterpillar and a spider on its web, on a cream background lightly painted with impressions of waratah leaves. The waratah leaves can be worked in two ways—as embroidered leaves all worked as flat embroidery, or as a combination of bonded appliqué shapes and raised wired fabric shapes.

Embroider the butterfly following the detailed instructions on pages 62–64.

Requirements

30 cm (12") square background fabric (I suggest a light colour as the butterfly does not show to its best advantage on dark fabrics)

30 cm (12") square pelon

30 cm (12") square backing fabric (calico, homespun or quilter's muslin)

20 cm (8") square olive-green cotton fabric (for bonded appliqué leaves)

15 cm (6") square quilter's muslin or homespun (for stitched leaves)

10 cm and 25 cm (4" and 10") hoops

15 cm x 30 cm (6" x 12") crimson-red lining fabric (a shade lighter than DMC 814)

2 pieces 15 cm (6") square Vliesofix or fusible web

15 cm (6") square silk screen fabric 10txxx or 2 pieces silk organza bonded together

34 gauge beading wire or fine silk covered wire (0.01" diameter) for butterfly wings

30 gauge paper covered wire for waratah bracts and leaves

30 gauge cotton covered wire for waratah flowerhead

black glass seed beads

black petite seed beads

PVA glue

flat brush

crimson-red watercolour pencil

threads

DMC Stranded Cotton: 310 (black), 936, 937 (olive-greens), 814, 816 (red), 309 (pink), 733 (yellow-green), 3371 (brown-black)

DMC Perle 5: 814 (red), 729 (golden brown)

20 cm DMC Soft Cotton no.4: grey or any dark colour, white or cream

Cifonda Silk: black, white, orange 135

dark brown chenille thread for butterfly body (optional)

metallic machine thread, Madeira 40 Astro-1 silver or gold

clear machine thread

needles

crewel 10, 8 and 6

hand appliqué 12

chenille 20

yarn darner

Stitches

Running stitch, stem stitch, chain stitch, satin stitch, ringed stitch, backstitch, straight stitch, bullion stitch

Method

Trace the design outline onto the backing fabric and place the backing fabric, pelon and background fabric into the 25 cm (10") hoop as described on page 12. Transfer the design to the background fabric with running stitch, using a single strand of olive-green stranded

This embroidery is worked on a cream poly satin background lightly watercoloured with impressions of waratah leaves

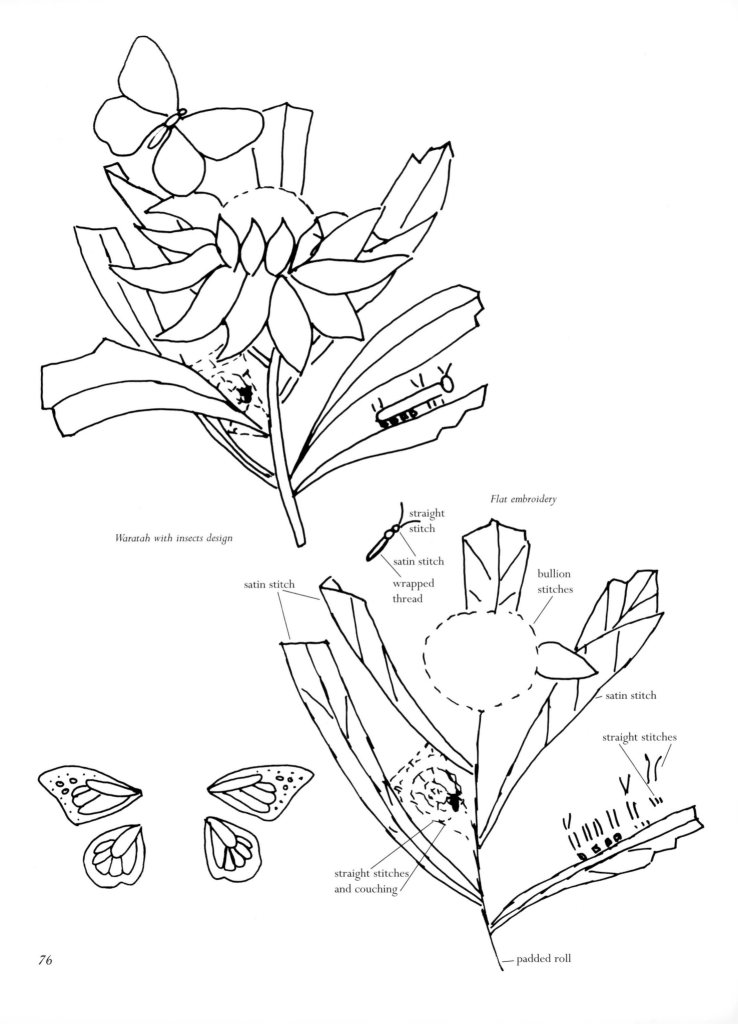

Waratah with insects design

Flat embroidery

straight stitch

satin stitch

wrapped thread

satin stitch

bullion stitches

satin stitch

straight stitches

straight stitches and couching

padded roll

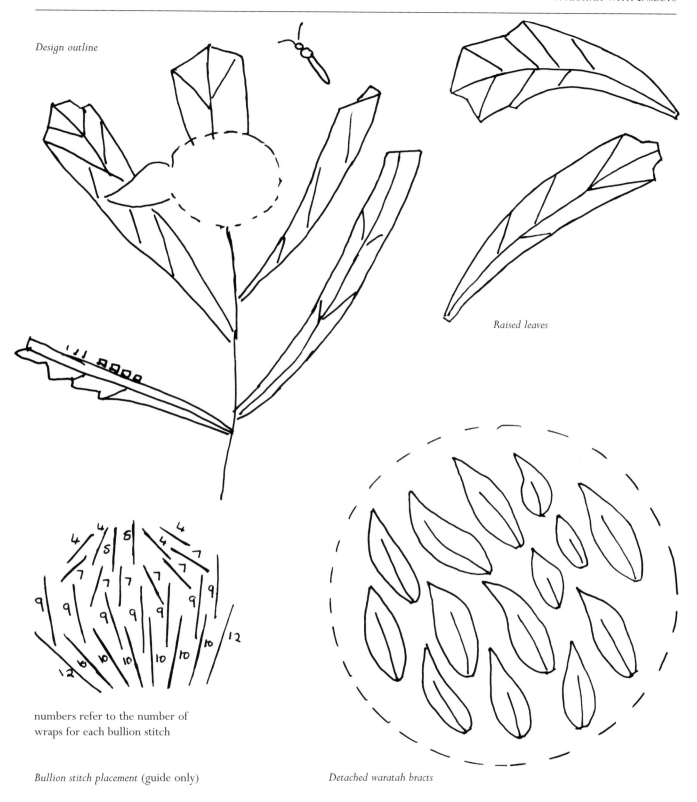

Design outline

Raised leaves

numbers refer to the number of
wraps for each bullion stitch

Bullion stitch placement (guide only)

Detached waratah bracts

cotton for the waratah stem and a single strand of crimson-red stranded thread for the waratah flowerhead. Mark the length of the butterfly body with a single strand of black stranded cotton.

If you are working the waratah leaves as part of the flat embroidery, use a single strand of olive-green stranded thread to work a row of running stitch inside the pencil line. Mark the veins as well as the outside of the leaves. If you are working the leaves as bonded appliqué work a running stitch down the vein lines only.

FLAT EMBROIDERY

For more detailed instructions on working the individual elements of waratah and butterfly, spider and caterpillar, refer to pages 42–46 and 61–65.

Stem

This is a padded roll worked in golden-brown Perle 5 (see page 44).

Stitched flat leaves

Backstitch around the leaf shape and along the central vein using a single strand of light olive-green stranded cotton. Work satin stitch in 2 strands of the dark olive-green stranded cotton to fill in the leaf shape. Bring the needle and thread up on the vein line and take them down on the outside of the backstitch.

Using a single strand of yellow-green stranded cotton work straight stitches for the side veins of the leaf.

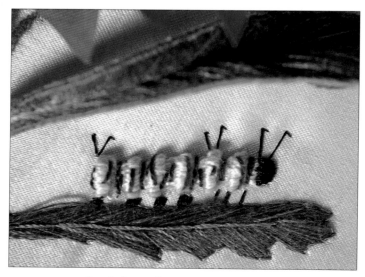

Detail of caterpillar

The central vein is 2 strands of yellow-green cotton couched in place with a single strand of yellow-green cotton.

Bonded flat leaves

Trace the reverse of the leaf shape onto the paper covering of the bonding fabric. Bond the traced shape onto the leaf fabric, carefully cut out the leaf and remove the paper. Place the cut-out shape onto the background fabric using the stitched vein lines as a placement guide and bond into position with the heat of the iron.

Couch 2 strands of light olive-green stranded cotton around the edge of the leaf with a single strand of matching cotton. Bring the needle out in the background fabric and take it down through the bonded fabric and the background fabric.

The central vein is 2 strands of yellow-green cotton couched in place with a single strand of the same coloured cotton; the side veins are straight stitches worked with a single strand of yellow-green cotton.

Waratah flowerhead, bullion stitches

The background fabric under the waratah flowerhead may be coloured with watercolour pencil. The flowerhead itself is worked in three stages.

In the first stage, the flowerhead is covered with loose untidy bullion stitches worked in red Perle 5. Use the diagram as a guide to placement. The bullion stitches at the base of the flowerhead should not be too closely packed, as you need to allow for positioning the wrapped threads and wired fingers over the bullions later.

Spider web and spider

The spider web appears between the 2 leaves on the left of the stem.

Using a short length of metallic thread in a crewel 8 needle, mark the outside boundaries of the web with long straight stitches, and couch them in place with the clear machine thread. Again in metallic thread, work straight stitches from the centre of the web to the outside boundaries. These stitches represent the spokes of the web. Any stitches longer than 10 mm ($^3/_8$") will need to be couched down.

Working from the centre of the web in the metallic thread, join the web spokes with straight stitches.

The spider's legs are worked in six groups of 2 chain stitches, using a single strand of black silk thread. One black seed beed and a petite glass bead represent the head and body. Position the spider so that it will not be covered by raised leaves or waratah bracts.

Caterpillar

The caterpillar sits on the lowest right hand leaf.

Use a single strand of black stranded cotton to work 3 straight stitches for the front legs and 4 blocks of satin stitch for the back legs.

Use the light coloured soft cotton to work the foundation stitches for the caterpillar's body. Work ringed backstitch over the foundation stitches in white stranded cotton. Bring the cotton out from under the head stitches and along the body.

Place some orange ringed backstitches along the top and bottom of the caterpillar's body.

Cover the head foundation stitches with black silk satin stitches and use the same thread to work the feelers and stripes.

Butterfly body

The abdomen takes up half the length of the butterfly's body. Take a length of dark soft cotton in from the front and leave a tail. Bring the cotton up again close to the tail of thread and make another tail. Wrap the 2 threads with a single strand of black-brown stranded cotton.

The head (one-third of the remaining length of the butterfly body) is padded satin stitch. The eyes are 2 petite glass beads. The area between the head and abdomen is not stitched until after the wings have been stitched in place.

Waratah flowerhead, wrapped threads

Follow the diagram on page 46 in placing the wrapped threads.

Working from the top of the flower to the stem, take 2 strands of red Perle 5 in from the front and bring them up again close to where you took them down. Wrap these 4 strands with 3 strands of dark red stranded cotton. Anchor all the threads securely on the back of the work under the flowerhead.

RAISED EMBROIDERY

The raised elements, attached when the flat embroidery is completed, include 18 wrapped wire fingers and 14 bracts for the waratah, 4 wings for the butterfly and 2 leaves.

Detail of butterfly. The feelers are straight stitches worked with a single strand of black stranded cotton

Waratah flowerhead, wrapped wire fingers

Cut 18 x 6 cm (2¼") lengths of 30 gauge cotton covered wire.

Wrap the centre 10 mm (³/₈") of each wire with 1 strand of pink stranded cotton. Fold the wire in half and tie 3 strands of red stranded cotton to one side. Wrap the doubled wire with the 3 strands, making 20–28 wraps, approximately 2.5 cm (1") long.

Waratah flowerhead, wired bracts

Trace the bract shapes onto a piece of the red lining fabric using a B pencil. Bond the 2 pieces of lining fabric and place in a hoop. Use a single strand of dark red stranded cotton and satin stitch to couch 34 gauge beading wire or fine covered wire down the centre of the bract.

Paint the bracts on both sides with a mixture of glue and water, allow to dry and cut out the shapes when you are ready to attach them to the embroidery.

Butterfly wings

Trace the wing shapes onto silk screen fabric or bonded silk organza, and work the embroidery following the instructions on pages 62–64.

Waratah leaves, embroidered

Trace the 2 leaf shapes onto calico or quilter's muslin with a B pencil. Couch 30 gauge paper covered wire down the central vein and around the outside of the leaf shape using a single strand of the light olive-green stranded cotton. Embroider inside the wire shape with satin stitch, using 2 strands of the same thread.

Satin stitch over the wire around the leaf, using 1 strand of the light olive-green stranded cotton. Work satin stitch over the wire down the centre vein using a single strand of the yellow-green stranded cotton, and work straight stitches with a single strand of the same thread to represent the side veins.

Cut out the shapes.

Alternative waratah leaves, wired fabric

Trace the leaf shapes onto cotton fabric of the appropriate colour.

Use 1 strand of the light olive-green stranded cotton to couch 30 gauge paper covered wire down the central vein and around the leaf shape.

Satin stitch over the wire around the shape using a single strand of the light olive-green stranded cotton.

Satin stitch over the central vein wire using a single strand of the yellow-green stranded cotton, and then work straight stitches in the same thread for the side veins.

Cut out the shapes.

ASSEMBLY

Attach the wrapped wire fingers for the waratah flowerhead in 2 rows, starting at the top of the flowerhead and working down using the photo on page 75 as a guide.

Position and attach the waratah bracts; first the bracts that stand away from the flowerhead, then the bracts that cover it. Do not shape them at this point—just lay them flat against the embroidery.

Position and attach the butterfly wings; first the 2 hind wings, then the fore wings.

Fill the butterfly's body (between the wings) with 1 or 2 straight stitches in dark brown chenille thread *or* 3 rows of cut turkey stitch worked with 6 strands of dark brown stranded cotton along the body.

Position and attach the raised leaves. You may need to add a few slip stitches along the length of the leaves to keep them in position.

Use tweezers to manipulate the waratah bracts into position.

The embroidery is now ready to mount and frame.

Chapter Fourteen

WILDFLOWER POSY II

THIS WILDFLOWER POSY features wattle with cylindrical flowerspikes, a waratah and bottlebrush.

Requirements

30 cm (12") square backing fabric
30 cm (12") square pelon
30 cm (12") square background fabric
15 cm x 30 cm (6" x 12") red lining fabric
15 cm (12") square fusible web (Vliesofix)
10 cm and 25 cm (4" and 10") hoops
20 cm x 12 mm olive-green satin ribbon
B pencil
PVA glue
flat brush
30 gauge cotton covered wire for waratah fingers
30 gauge paper covered wire for waratah leaves
34 gauge beading wire or fine silk covered wire for waratah bracts
threads
    DMC stranded cottons: 3787 (taupe), 936 (olive-green), 743 (bright yellow), 435 (tan), 321 (crimson), 666 (red), 814 (dark garnet red), 733 (yellow-green)
    DMC Perle 5: 814 (garnet red), 729 (gold-brown)
    DMC Perle 8: (red-brown)
    Cifonda Silk: 492 or 523 (green)
    DMC Flower Thread: 936 (olive-green)
needles
    crewel 10, 8 and 5
    chenille 20
    hand appliqué 12
    tapestry 22 or 24
    yarn darner or large chenille

Method

Trace the design outline onto the backing fabric and place backing fabric, pelon and background fabric into the 25 cm (10") hoop as described on page 12. Transfer the design to the background fabric with running stitch using a single strand of thread in the following colours:
    wattle and waratah stems—tan stranded cotton
    bottlebrush stem—taupe stranded cotton
    waratah leaf—olive-green stranded cotton
    leaf line—green silk

FLAT EMBROIDERY

Work the embroidery in the order given, completing the flat embroidery before adding the raised pieces.

Wattle

Using the red-brown Perle 8, work stem stitch along the stem lines, then whip the stem stitch with a single strand of tan stranded cotton.

Using the photograph as a guide, work feather (or fly) stitch along the leaf line with a single strand of the green silk thread. Work the arms of the stitches close together.

Work the wattle buds in French knots, using 3 strands of bright yellow stranded cotton.

Bottlebrush

Work chain stitch along the stem lines using 2 strands of taupe, 1 strand of olive-green and 1 strand of tan stranded cotton all together in a chenille 20 needle.

Whip the chain stitches with 1 strand of taupe and 1 strand of olive-green stranded cotton.

Completed posy with wattle, waratah and bottlebrush

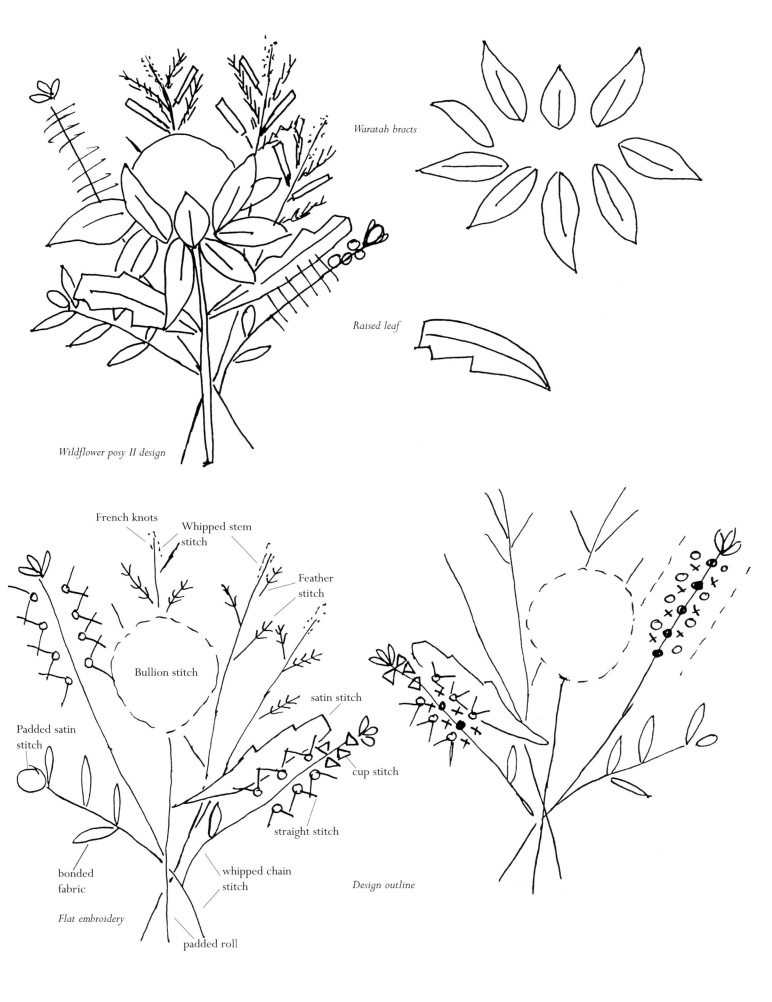

Waratah bracts

Raised leaf

Wildflower posy II design

French knots

Whipped stem
stitch

Feather
stitch

Bullion stitch

Padded satin
stitch

satin stitch

cup stitch

straight stitch

bonded
fabric

whipped chain
stitch

Design outline

Flat embroidery

padded roll

At the tip of the leaf stem on the lower left mark an oval shape to represent the leaf tip.

Outline the oval in backstitch, using a single strand of tan stranded cotton.

Work 2 or 3 padding stitches inside the shape with 3 strands of tan stranded cotton.

Cover the padding stitches with satin stitches, working from the tip of the leaf bud to the stem with a single strand of tan stranded cotton.

Place 1 strand of yellow, 3 strands of red and 3 strands of crimson stranded cotton in a large needle and work the flat stitches for the bottlebrush indicated by the symbol ⅄ (see page 49).

Wrap the bases of the red and yellow threads with olive-green flower thread before fanning out the threads.

Waratah

The stem of the waratah is a padded roll (see pagr 44) made with a foundation of 5 lengths of gold-brown Perle 5; this is stitched in place with another length of the same thread.

Outline the flat waratah leaf with backstitch using a strand of olive-green stranded cotton. Fill the shape with satin stitch using 2 strands of olive-green stranded cotton, taking the needle and thread down outside the backstitch and up on the stem line. The side veins are straight stitches worked in a single strand of yellow-green stranded cotton, while the central vein is 2 strands of yellow-green stranded cotton couched in place with a single strand of the same thread.

Waratah flowerhead

The first layer is untidy bullions worked in garnet red Perle 5. Follow the diagram on page 46 for stitch placement.

The second layer is wrapped threads. Take 2 strands of garnet red Perle 5 in from the front of the work, leaving a 10 cm (4") tail of thread at the front; bring the thread up close by to leave a matching tail. Wrap these 4 strands tightly with 3 strands of dark garnet red stranded cotton. Follow the diagram on page 46 to place the wrapped threads.

Bottlebrush

Work bottlebrush tips as 3 groups of chain stitches worked on top of each other (see page 49). Work the central group first, then a group on either side, using 1

strand of olive-green and 1 strand of tan stranded cotton. The stitches are 6 mm (¼") long.

The buds at the tip of the right hand stem are worked in cup stitch. Use the olive-green flower thread to embroider 5 or 6 buds.

Use 4 strands of red, 3 strands of crimson and 1 strand of yellow stranded cotton, with 1 strand of olive-green flower thread in another needle, to work the tufts of stamens along the stem indicated by the symbols ✕ and ● (see page 83).

Bottlebrush flat leaves

Bond 10 cm (4") of ribbon to Vliesofix and cut out 5 bottlebrush leaf shapes. Bond the leaves in position on the background fabric, placing a layer of Gladbake between the iron and the fabric to protect the iron (see page 15).

Use a single strand of olive-green stranded thread to work a row of backstitch down the vein lines.

Bottlebrush leaves

RAISED EMBROIDERY

These elements are worked separately and attached to the work when the flat embroidery is complete.

Wattle

The wattle flowers are worked as applied slips on calico, cut out and attached to the embroidery with slip stitch. A few French knots may need to be added to cover where slip and embroidery meet (see pages 30–31).

Waratah flowerhead

You will need to make 18 wired fingers, which are attached in rows (see pages 45–46). Attach the row closest to the top of the waratah first, then the row near the stem.

Waratah bracts

Trace the bract shapes onto a piece of red lining fabric, bond the 2 layers of lining fabric together and place in a hoop with the traced bract shapes facing you. Stitch a length of fine wire doubled down each central vein. Paint the bracts on both sides with 80% glue, 20% water, and allow to dry.

Cut out the bracts and attach to the embroidery, first placing the 5 bracts standing free of the flowerhead, then the 3 standing against it.

Waratah leaf

The waratah leaf is a detached embroidered wired shape.

Couch the 30 gauge paper covered wire down the central vein and around the outside of the leaf with a single strand of olive-green stranded cotton. Fill inside the wired shape with satin stitch worked with 2 strands of olive-green stranded cotton, then satin stitch over the wire around the leaf with 1 strand of the same thread.

Use 1 strand of yellow-green stranded cotton to satin stitch over the wire down the centre of the leaf, and work straight stitches with 1 strand of the same thread to represent the side veins.

Cut out the leaf and attach it to the work.

Bottlebrush leaves

These 3 leaves are detached glued fabric leaves.

Work a backstitch using 1 strand of olive-green cotton along the centre of the green satin ribbon for the mid vein. Leave a 12 cm (5") tail of thread at one end to attach the leaf to the embroidery.

Paint the stitched ribbon with 80% glue, 20% water, and allow to dry. Cut out the leaf shapes and stitch the leaves along the bottlebrush stem.

Trim the bottlebrush tufts to about 5 mm (¼") length. Use tweezers to manipulate the waratah fingers and bracts into a pleasing arrangement.

Chapter Fifteen

WILDFLOWER POSY III

Requirements

30 cm (12") square backing fabric

30 cm (12") square pelon

30 cm (12") square background fabric

15 cm (6") square Vilene (non-iron-on interfacing) for
tea-tree petals

8 cm (3") square doctor flannel or cream wool fabric
for the flannel flower

15 cm (5") square firm iron-on interfacing for the flannel flower

15 cm (5") square calico or quilter's muslin for the wattle
spikes

10 cm and 15 cm (4" and 10") hoops

10 cm x 12 mm (4" x ½") olive-green satin ribbon

1 cm x 8 cm (³/₈" x 3") cardboard

HB pencil

34 gauge beading wire or very fine silk covered wire

paper

embroidery scissors

PVA glue

threads

   DMC Stranded Cottons: 3787 (taupe), 744 (yellow),
3347 (green-yellow), ecru or 712 (cream), 666
(crimson), 321 (red), 936 (olive-green), 435 (tan),
224 and 223 (pink) 3721 (dark pink)

   DMC Perle 8: 918 (red-brown)

   DMC Perle 5: 725 (yellow)

   DMC Flower Thread: 936 (olive-green)

   Appleton's Crewel Wool: 342 (grey-green)

   Cifonda Silk: 492 or 523 (green)

   DMC Soft Cotton no.4: grey or light green

needles

   crewel 10, 8 and 5

hand appliqué 12

chenille 20

tapestry 22

yarn darner

Method

Trace the design outline onto the backing fabric and place
the backing fabric, pelon and background fabric into the
25 cm (10") hoop as described on page 12. Transfer the
design to the background fabric with running stitch using a single strand of thread in the following colours:

   wattle stem—tan stranded cotton

   leaf line—green silk

   bottlebrush, tea-tree and flannel flower stems—
taupe stranded cotton

   tea-tree flower centres, tea-tree bud—pink stranded
cotton

FLAT EMBROIDERY

Work the flat embroidery in the order given, completing it before adding the raised pieces.

Wattle

Work a row of stem stitch along the stem line in red-
brown Perle 8 and whip with a single strand of tan
stranded cotton.

   Use a single strand of one of the Cifonda green silk
threads to work a feather stitch or Y (fly) stitch along
the leaf line. Work the arms of the feather stitch close
together.

   Wattle buds are French knots worked with the yellow Perle 5 thread.

Wildflower posy of fluffy wattle, tea-tree blossoms, bottlebrush and flannel flower

Bottlebrush

Work chain stitch along the stem line using 2 strands of taupe stranded cotton with 1 strand of olive-green and 1 strand of tan together in a crewel 5 needle.

Whip the chain stitches with 1 strand of taupe and 1 strand of olive-green stranded cotton.

At the tip of the unflowered leaf stem mark an oval shape to represent the leaf tip, using backstitch with a single strand of tan stranded cotton to outline it on the right side of the work. Work 2 or 3 padding stitches across the shape, within the backstitch outline, using 3 strands of tan stranded cotton. Work over the padding stitches, from the tip to the stem, with a satin stitch in 2 strands of tan stranded cotton.

Using 1 strand of yellow, 3 strands of red and 3 strands of crimson stranded cotton in a large needle, work the flat stitches for the bottlebrush (see page 49). Wrap the base of the threads with the olive-green flower thread before fanning out the separate strands.

Tea-tree

Using 3 strands of taupe stranded cotton, work a row of Portuguese stem stitch along the stem line.

The tea-tree leaves are thin and pointed, worked as 3 straight stitches with a single strand of olive-green stranded cotton. Work the central stitch first, then work a slightly shorter stitch on either side fanning out from the stem. Use the photograph as a guide.

The bud is a padded satin stitch shape. Fill the outline with 3 padding stitches worked in soft cotton; cover the padding stitches with satin stitch worked with a single strand of pink stranded cotton. Stitches are worked from the stem to the tip. Use 2 strands of olive-green stranded cotton to work diagonal stitches over the pink satin stitch to represent the bud sepals.

Use either satin stitch or French knots worked with 1 strand of the dark pink cotton to fill the centre of the tea-tree flower. This can be done now or left until the raised petals have been attached.

Flannel flower

The flannel flower stem is worked in wrapped threads. Take a strand of soft cotton in from the front at the base of the stem, leaving a 15 cm (6") tail of thread, and bring it out again as close as possible to the same spot with another 15 cm (6") tail of thread. Wrap the 2 tails of thread with the crewel wool for the length of the

stem and couch stem in position with a second strand of crewel wool.

Bottlebrush

Use the olive-green flower thread to work 5 or 6 needlewoven cup stitches at the tip of the partly opened bottlebrush flowerhead. Use 4 strands of red, 3 strands of crimson and 1 strand of yellow stranded cotton in a chenille 20 needle to work the open flower stamens (tufts) along the bottlebrush stems. Work the leaning tufts before the upright ones.

RAISED EMBROIDERY

Make these elements separately and attach them once the flat embroidery has been completed.

Wattle

Although the photograph shows fluffy wattle, you may prefer to embroider cylindrical flowerspikes. If you are using fluffy wattle, make 8–10 balls using the yellow Perle 5.

Cylindrical wattle spikes are made as slips on a piece of calico or quilter's muslin (see pages 30–31). Draw 3 lines 12 mm (½") long and 2 lines 5 mm (¼") long along the grain of the fabric, with 2 cm (¾") space between the lines. Work over each line with 3 straight stitches the length of the line, using 1 strand of green stranded cotton and 2 strands of yellow stranded cotton. With 2 strands of yellow stranded cotton work French knots over the straight stitches.

Work a running stitch around each shape 2 mm ($^1/_{16}$") away from the embroidery and paint outside the running stitch with Fray-Stoppa. Cut out the shapes and draw up the running stitch.

Attach the fluffy balls or the wattle slips to the embroidery.

Tea-tree

Make 10 detached embroidered wired petal shapes on the non-iron-on interfacing (see pages 52–53) and cut them out. Mark 5 equal divisions around each tea-tree flower centre and attach a petal at each mark. Lay the petals flat.

Stamens can be worked around the outside of the flower centre using 2 strands of green stranded cotton to work a row of cut turkey stitch. Paint the loops with PVA glue and trim when dry.

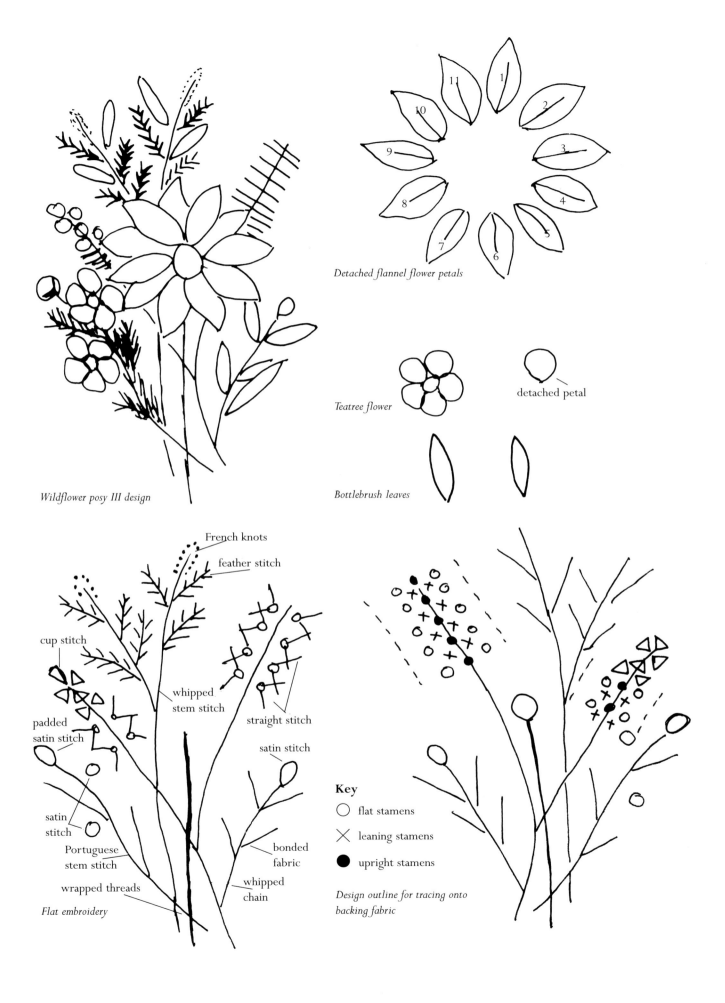

Wildflower posy III design

Detached flannel flower petals

11 1
10 2
9 3
8 4
7 5
6

Teatree flower

detached petal

Bottlebrush leaves

French knots

feather stitch

cup stitch

whipped
stem stitch

straight stitch

padded
satin stitch

satin stitch

satin
stitch

Portuguese
stem stitch

wrapped threads

bonded
fabric

whipped
chain

Flat embroidery

Key

◯ flat stamens

✕ leaning stamens

● upright stamens

*Design outline for tracing onto
backing fabric*

Flannel flower

Trace the flannel flower petal shapes onto the non-shiny side of the iron-on interfacing. Bond the interfacing and the doctor flannel (or wool fabric) together.

Satin stitch doubled fine wire down the centre of each petal with 1 strand of cream cotton.

Cut out the petal shapes and paint the edges with a mixture of 75% glue, 25% water. Allow to dry, then attach the petal shapes around the flannel flower centre, laying them flat against the work.

The flannel flower centre is a fluffy wattle ball made with 3 strands of crewel wool and 6 strands of cream stranded cotton, trimmed to 5 mm (¼").

Bottlebrush leaves

Work 5 separate 15 mm (⁵/₈") lines of backstitch along the centre of the satin ribbon, leaving a 12 cm (5") tail of cotton at one end of each backstitched line. The backstitch represents the mid veins of the leaves.

Paint the satin ribbon on both sides with a mixture of 80% glue, 20% water, and allow to dry. Cut out the leaf shapes and attach them to the work using the tails of cotton.

FINAL TOUCHES

Cut the bottlebrush tufts to length. Use tweezers to arrange the petals of the tea-tree, the flannel flower and the bottlebrush leaves.

Your project is now ready for mounting.

Chapter Sixteen

WREATH OF WILDFLOWERS

A RICHNESS of wildflowers including flannel flowers, fluffy wattle, cylindrical wattle spikes, bluebells, bottlebrush, gum blossom and gumnuts, tea-tree and waratah. You'll also find a lucky spider on its web.

Requirements

35 cm (14") square backing fabric

35 cm (14") square pelon

35 cm (14") square background fabric

10 cm and 30 cm (4" and 12") hoops

15 cm (6") square calico or quilter's muslin for detached gum leaf and wattle spikes

2 x 8 cm (3") squares doctor flannel for the flannel flower

2 x 15 cm (6") squares firm iron-on interfacing for the flannel flower

10 cm x 12 mm (4" x ½") olive-green satin ribbon

10 cm x 12 mm (4" x ½") fusible web (Vliesofix)

1 cm x 8 cm thin cardboard (cereal box) for the wattle balls

1.5 cm x 8 cm (⅝" x 3") thin cardboard (cereal box) for the gum blossom

15 cm (6") non iron-on interfacing for the tea-tree flowers

4 cm x 10 cm (1½" x 4") brown felt for the gumnuts

34 gauge beading wire (or 0.01" silk covered fine wire) for flannel flower and waratah bracts

30 gauge paper covered wire for detached gum leaf

30 gauge cotton covered wire for waratah fingers

3 mm (⅛") cardboard disc (from a hole punch)

soft sheet nail 1.6 mm diameter

Matisse folk art paint in Antique White and Antique Green

white PVA glue

threads

DMC stranded cotton: 444 (yellow), 321 (crimson), 666 (red), 936 (olive-green), 733 (light olive-green), 3787 (taupe), 345 (tan), 3347 (yellow-green), 3346 (light yellow-green), 792 (blue), 814 (dark garnet red), 816 (garnet red), 309 (pink), 223 (pink), 3721 (dark pink), 502 (blue-green), 503 (light blue-green), 839 (mid-brown), 841 (light brown), ecru or 712 (cream)

DMC Perle 5: 727, 744 (yellows)

DMC Perle 8: 918 (red-brown)

Cifonda Silk: 115 (pink) or 1115 (cream), 792 (green), white

DMC Flower Thread: 936 (green)

DMC Soft Cotton no.4: 839 or 841 (brown)

needles

crewel 10, 8 and 5

tapestry 22 and 26

chenille 20

hand appliqué 12

yarn darner

Stitches

Running stitch, backstitch, feather stitch, chain stitch, whipping, cup stitch, straight stitch, tufting, needlewoven picot, satin stitch, French knots, needlewoven picot, detached buttonhole stitch, Portuguese stem stitch, wrapped threads

Method

Trace the design outline on to the backing fabric and place the backing fabric, pelon and background fabric in the 30 cm (12") hoop as described on page 12.

The background of the wildflower wreath is cream poly satin lightly printed with impressions of maidenhair fern leaves to soften the line between the fabric and the embroidery. A circular area slightly larger than the area covered by the embroidery was printed using maidenhair fern leaves coated with folk art paint (a little black worked into yellow oxide and mixed with textile medium)

Wreath of wildflowers design

Wildflower wreath flat embroidery

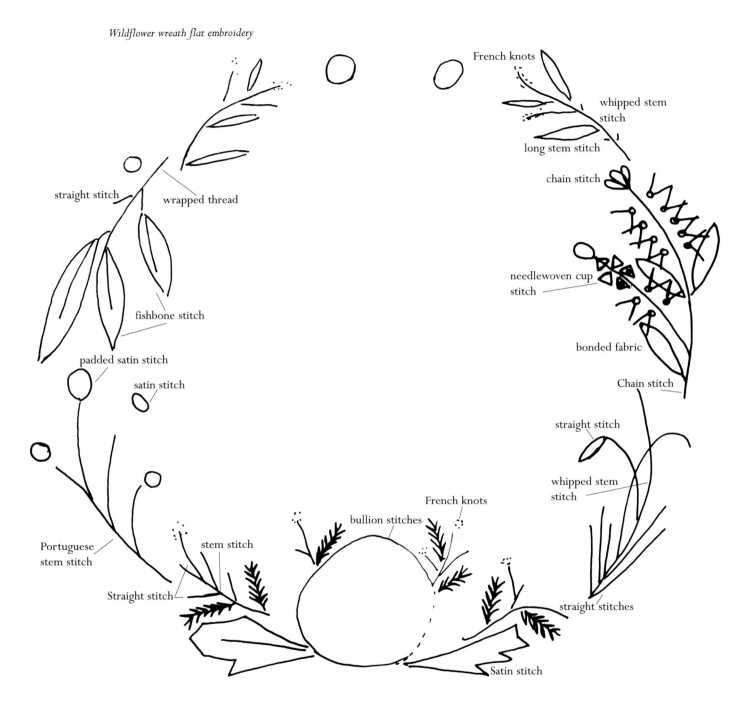

Transfer the design to the background fabric in running stitch using a single strand of stranded cotton in the following colours:

wattle stems and bluebell stems—tan
bottlebrush and tea-tree stems—taupe
gum stem—light brown
waratah and bottlebrush leaves—olive-green (work

inside pencil lines for waratah leaves; work central vein only for bottlebrush leaves)
spiky wattle leaves, flannel flower centres—yellow-green (work inside pencil line for leaves)
tea-tree flower centres and bud—pink
waratah flowerhead—garnet red
fluffy wattle leaves—green silk

Design outline

Key

○ flat stamens

✕ leaning tufts

● straight tufts

FLAT EMBROIDERY

Waratah leaves

Work backstitch around the leaf shape, outside the running stitch, in a single strand of olive-green stranded cotton. Fill the shape with satin stitch using 2 strands of olive-green cotton. It may help to put in some directional stitches first. Satin stitches cover the backstitch.

Use 1 strand of light olive-green cotton and straight stitch to work the veins of the leaf.

Fluffy wattle

Work stem stitch along the stem line with the red-brown Perle 8 and whip it with 1 strand of tan stranded cotton.

The flower stalks are represented by straight stitches worked with red-brown Perle 8.

Work feather stitch along the stem line for the leaves in a single strand of green silk. Work the arms of the feather stitch close together.

The wattle buds are groups of French knots worked in yellow Perle 5.

Cylindrical wattle spikes

Work stem stitch along the stem line in 2 strands of tan stranded cotton and whip with 2 strands of tan stranded cotton.

Backstitch around the leaf shape with a single strand of yellow-green stranded cotton. Working from the outside of the leaf shape to the centre with a single strand of yellow-green stranded cotton, fill the leaf shape with long stem stitch.

The wattle buds are groups of French knots worked with 2 strands of yellow stranded cotton.

Tea-tree

The side branches are worked in Portuguese stem stitch using 2 strands of taupe stranded cotton. The main stem is also worked in Portuguese stem stitch, using 4 strands of taupe stranded cotton.

The leaves are worked as groups of 3 straight stitches with a single strand of olive-green stranded cotton. The central stitch is longer than the other two and they all fan out from the same place on the stem.

The bud is padded satin stitch. Use soft cotton to work 3 straight stitches side by side across the bud shape. Cover the padding stitches with satin stitch worked with a single strand of pink stranded cotton. Run the stitches from the stem to the tip of the bud.

Make some diagonal stitches over the pink stitches in 1 strand of olive-green stranded cotton to represent the bud sepals.

Bluebells

Embroider the back stems first, working a row of stem stitch in red-brown Perle 8 thread. Untidily whip the stem stitch with 2 strands of yellow-green stranded cotton, allowing some of the red-brown to show through.

Work the bluebell leaves in long straight stitches using 2 strands of yellow-green stranded cotton.

The bud is worked with 1 strand of blue stranded cotton. Make a long straight stitch the length of the bud; continue, making long straight stitches coming in and out of the same place and alternating the cotton from side to side. Work in this manner until the bud is a nice shape, about 9 stitches in total.

Yellow-green straight stitches at the base of the bud form the sepals.

Gum blossom and leaves

The gum stem is wrapped threads. Take a thread of soft cotton no.4 in from the front, leaving a 12 cm (5") tail of thread. Bring the thread up close to where it went in, leaving a second 12 cm (5") tail on the front of the work. Wrap the 2 tails of thread with a single strand of brown stranded cotton for 2.5 cm (1") until the wrapped threads are 10 mm (³/₈") shorter than the division in the branch.

Couch the wrapped thread in place with a second strand of brown cotton. Join in a second wrapping strand and wrap and couch the 2 threads until the branch division is reached.

Separate the 2 threads of soft cotton and wrap them individually to form the leaf stalks. Couch the leafstalks in position and take the soft cotton thread to the back inside the leaf shape.

Make straight stitches using 2 strands of brown stranded cotton to represent the single leaf stem and the stem to the side view tassel.

Work a row of backstitch around each leaf shape using 1 strand of dark blue-green stranded cotton. Fill the leaves with fishbone stitch in 2 strands of the dark blue-green stranded cotton. The first stitch of the fishbone stitch is half the length of the leaf.

Work the leaf veins in 1 strand of the light brown stranded cotton.

To start the gum blossom, position the cardboard disc for the centre and stitch a cross over it with 1 strand of any green stranded cotton, then work satin stitch over the disc diagonally, from one quarter to the opposite quarter, with 1 strand of green stranded cotton.

Work 2 rows of cut turkey stitch around the covered disc with 6 strands of pink or cream silk. Stitches on the first row are worked with the loops over the centre of the flower, while the stitches on the second row are worked with the loops away from the centre. Tie all the loops together.

Bottlebrush

Work chain stitch along the stem lines, using 2 strands of taupe and 1 strand of olive-green stranded cotton.

The leaves at the tip of the open brush stem are worked as 3 long chain stitches in 2 strands of olive-green stranded cotton. The tip of the partly opened brush is an oval shape worked in satin stitch using 1 strand of tan stranded cotton.

To start the leaves, bond some fusible web to 5 cm (2") of the green satin ribbon, cut out 3 leaf shapes and bond them to the embroidery, using the leaf vein lines as a guide to position. Work a backstitch with a single strand of olive-green cotton along the vein of each bonded leaf (see page 15).

The buds are worked as raised cup stitch using olive-green flower thread, on base stitches 3–4 mm (about $^1/_8$") long. The buds nearest the open brushes can have a loop of red threads coming out of the cup to show they are partly opened.

The flat stamens (indicated by o on the design outline) are worked with 3 strands of crimson, 4 strands of red and 1 strand of yellow stranded cotton. Bring the threads to the front 2 mm ($^1/_{16}$") from the stem line and wrap the whole group of threads 3 times with green flower thread. Fan out the group of red and yellow threads and take them singly to the back of the work.

Regroup the threads and work the next flat stamen.

Waratah

The waratah flowerhead is worked in layers (see page 98).

Layer 1: Bullion stitches—Work loose untidy bullions with garnet red Perle 5 following the suggested placement diagram. Leave spaces between the bullions at the base of the flowerhead.

Layer 2: Wrapped threads—Take 2 strands of garnet red Perle 5 in from the front, leaving a tail of thread on the front. Bring the threads up close to where they went down. Wrap these 4 threads with 3 strands of dark garnet red stranded cotton for the length required. Work 9 groups of wrapped threads, following the diagram for placement.

End off all threads on the back of the work under the flowerhead.

If you wish to include a spiderweb and spider work them at this stage (see pages 63–65).

RAISED EMBROIDERY

These raised elements are worked on the background fabric.

Bluebells

Mark a 3 mm ($^1/_8$") circle on the background fabric for the centre of the bluebell, tracing around the inside of a circle cut in card with a hole punch. Mark 5 equal divisions around the circle in B pencil.

Work a needlewoven picot across 2 adjoining divisions for each bluebell petal, using 3 strands of blue stranded cotton (see pages 21 and 58). Repeat to make 5 petals for each bluebell.

Work 3 French knots in the centre of each flower in 2 strands of white silk.

Bottlebrush

Work the leaning and upright bottlebrush tufts, indicated by ● and ✕ on the diagram, using 4 strands of red, 3 strands of crimson and 1 strand of yellow stranded cotton (see page 49). Do not cut the tufts at this stage.

RAISED PIECES

Waratah

Make 18 wired fingers for the waratah using 8 cm (3") lengths of 30 gauge cotton covered wire. Wrap the centre 10 mm ($^3/_8$") with 1 strand of dark pink stranded cotton. Fold the wire in half and wrap together with 3 strands of garnet red stranded cotton for the length required, generally between 22 and 27 wraps.

Attach the fingers to the work in 2 rows, working from the top down to the stem (see pages 45–46).

Trace the shapes of the bracts for the waratah onto red lining fabric. Bond this to another piece of red

Suggested bullion stitch placement

Suggested number of wraps (left to right)
Row 1: 4, 4, 5, 4, 4, 4.
Row 2: 8, 7, 7, 8, 9, 8, 7, 7, 8.
Row 3: 9, 9, 8, 9, 8, 8, 9, 9.
Row 4: 10, 6, 6, 5, 6, 6, 10.

Suggested wrapped thread placement

Raised embroidery

Flannel flower

Waratah bracts

Wired tea tree petal

Gum leaf

Wattle leaves

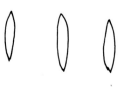

Detail of the waratah from the wildflower wreath

lining fabric and place in a 10 cm (4") hoop with the tracing face up.

Use 1 strand of garnet red stranded cotton to satin stitch doubled 34 gauge beading wire or fine wire down the centre vein.

Paint the fabric on both sides with a mixture of 80% glue, 20% water, and allow to dry. Cut out the shapes and attach them to the embroidery, folding them back flat against the background fabric.

Fluffy wattle

Make 11 fluffy wattle balls using both the Perle 5 yellow threads. Trim the threads so that the strands are no more than 4 mm (³/₁₆") long.

Tea-tree

I have used needlelace flowers here. Make 3 full flowers and 1 flower with only 3 petals (see page 54). Use 1 strand of the dark pink stranded cotton for the centres and 1 strand of pink cotton for the petals.

If you prefer, you can make 18 detached embroidered petal shapes using a single strand of pink cotton (see page 52). Attach the flowers to the background fabric, and fill the centres with satin stitch worked with a single strand of dark pink stranded cotton.

Stamens can be added to either type of flower if you wish by working a row of cut turkey stitch around the centre in 1 strand of green cotton. Paint the loops with glue and trim when they are dry.

Gumnuts, gum blossom and leaf

Referring to page 36, make 1 full and 1 half gumnut. Use 2 strands of taupe, 1 strand of light brown and 1 strand of brown stranded cotton to cover the felt beads. Attach the gumnuts to the background fabric and wrap the visible gumnut stalk with 1 strand of light brown stranded cotton.

The gum leaf is a detached embroidered wired shape. Trace the leaf onto calico or quilter's muslin and place the fabric in a small hoop. Use a single strand of light blue-green stranded cotton to couch 30 gauge paper covered wire down the central vein and around the edge of the shape. Fill the shape inside the wire with fishbone stitch worked with 2 strands of light blue-green stranded cotton. Satin stitch around the leaf with a single strand of light blue-green stranded cotton.

Cut out the leaf and attach it, wrapping the wire stalk with 1 strand of light brown stranded cotton.

To make the side view gum blossom, wrap 6 strands of pink or yellow silk in a V around a piece of cardboard 15 mm ($^5/_8$") wide. Tie at the top with 2 strands of green stranded cotton and remove from the cardboard. Tie 2 strands of green stranded cotton around the tassel about 2 mm ($^1/_{16}$") down from the top, and attach to the background fabric using the tails of the tying threads.

Cover the top of the tassel with green satin stitch.

Detached bottlebrush leaf

Work a line of backstitch 20 mm (¾") along the centre of the satin ribbon. Leave a tail of thread 12 cm (5") long at one end. Paint the ribbon on both sides with a mixture of 80% glue and 20% water. Allow to dry. Cut out a leaf shape and stitch it in position with the tail of thread.

Cylindrical wattle flowerspikes

The 5 cylindrical wattle flowerspikes are applied slips worked on calico. Mark 5 lines of different lengths, between 12 and 15 mm (about ½") long, on the calico in B pencil, following the grain of the fabric and leaving a 2 cm (¾") space between the lines. Use 1 strand of yellow-green and 2 strands of yellow stranded cotton to work 3 long stitches side by side the length of the pencilled lines. Cover these stitches with French knots worked with 2 strands of yellow stranded cotton.

Work a row of running stitch around the shape, about 2 mm ($^1/_{16}$") away from the embroidery and paint outside the running stitch with glue. Cut out the shape and pull up the running stitch.

Attach the slips to the background fabric with slip stitches.

Detached wattle leaves

Trace the shapes for the 3 detached wattle leaves onto the organza and place the organza and 2 layers of Solvy in a hoop. Backstitch around the leaf shapes with 1 strand of yellow-green stranded cotton and fill them with long stem stitch worked with 1 strand of yellow-green stranded cotton. Leave a 10 cm (4") tail of thread at the stalk end of the leaf.

Cut away the organza close to the embroidery and cut away the Solvy, leaving 1 mm of Solvy around the shape. Dunk the shape quickly in water and allow to dry.

Attach to the work using the tail of thread.

Flannel flowers

Trace the petal shapes for 2 flannel flowers onto the non-shiny side of the iron-on interfacing. Bond the flannel fabric to the interfacing and place the bonded fabrics in a hoop. Use 1 strand of cream stranded cotton to satin stitch doubled fine wire down the vein of each petal.

Cut out the petals and paint the edges a pale green colour, mixing a little Antique Green paint into Antique White.

Mix equal quantities of the pale green paint and glue together with a little water. Allow to dry and attach the petals to the background fabric.

The flannel flower centres are fluffy wattle balls made with 2 strands of grey-green wool and 4 strands of cream stranded cotton.

Finishing touches

Trim the bottlebrush tufts to length.

Moisten and trim the threads of the open gum blossom.

Cut some of the threads of the side view gum tassel.

Use tweezers to manipulate the wired fingers on the waratah, the waratah bracts, the gum leaf and the flannel flower petals into position.

The work is now ready for mounting.

Bibliography

My passion for reading and collecting books is almost as great as my need to be stitching. I have listed here only the books I have consulted while writing and researching this book.

Plant references

A Popular Guide to Wildflowers of NSW, Books 1 and 2: Florence Sulman, Angus and Robertson, Sydney 1913, 1914. These books were given to me by my paternal grandmother, who loved the Australian bush and planted many native plants in her garden.

Wild Flowers of Australia: Thistle Y. Harris, Angus & Robertson, Sydney 1947.

Key Guide to Australian Wildflowers: Leonard Cronin, Reed Books, Sydney 1987.

Australia's Native Flowers: Ken Stepnell & Teresa James, National Book Distributors and Publishers, Sydney 1986.

Gum Leaves and Geckoes: Gould League Nature Diary, The Gould League of Victoria, Melbourne.

Stitch and general embroidery books

The Stitches of Creative Embroidery: Jacqueline Enthoven, Reinhold Publishing Corporation, New York 1964.

Lalla Ward's Countryside Embroidery Book: Lalla Ward, Pelham Books, London 1989.

Wildflower Embroidery: Annette Rich, Milner Craft Series, Sydney 1994.

Australian Flora in Art from the Museum of Applied Arts and Sciences, Sydney: Margaret Betteridge, Sun Academy Series, Sydney 1979.

Needlework in Australia: Marion Fletcher, Oxford University Press, Melbourne 1989.

The Gentle Arts—200 Years of Australian Women's Domestic and Decorative Arts: Jennifer Isaacs, Lansdowne Press, Sydney 1987.

Australian Enquiry Book of General and Household Information: Mrs Lance Rawson, first published 1894, facsimile edition, Kangaroo Press, Sydney 1984.

Stumpwork: Historical & Contemporary Raised Embroidery: Muriel Best, Batsford, London 1987.

Suppliers

The threads, needles, hoops and beads used in the text are available from needlework shops. Fabrics and pelon on which the designs are worked, are available at patchwork or dress fabric shops, as is Vliesofix (fusible web) and the interfacings used. Craft supply shops stock the PVA glue and wire. Wire used in the projects can be found at cake decorating supply shops. For information about your nearest supplier please contact the following:

DMC Threads

Australia

DMC Needlecraft Pty Ltd
51–55 Carrington Road
Marrickville NSW 2204
Ph (02) 9559 3088

New Zealand

Warnaar Trading Co. Ltd
PO Box 19567
Christchurch 8003
Free phone 0800 800

United States of America

The DMC Corporation
10 Port Kearny
South Kearney NJ 07032
Ph (201) 589 0606   Fax (201) 589 8931

United Kingdom

DMC Creative World
Pullman Road, Wigston
Leicestershire LE18 2DY
Ph (116) 281 1040   Fax (201) 589 8931

Cifonda Threads

PO Ravenshoe
Queensland 4872
Ph (07) 4097 0108

I am able to obtain my supplies from the following retail outlets. Mail order is available from these outlets.

Threads, needles, hoops and needlework supplies:

The Crewel Gobelin
9 Marian Street
Killara NSW 2071
Ph (02) 9498 6831   Fax (02) 9499 5001

Victoria House Needlecraft
Main Street
Mittagong NSW 2575
Ph (02) 4871 1682   Fax (02) 4871 2611

Wire

Cake Decorators Supplies
Shop 1, 770 George Street
Sydney NSW 2000
Ph (02) 9212 4050

All materials required for the projects may be obtained in kit form, through mail order. Please write for information and price list:

Australian Nature Designs
'Kelmar'
Scarlett Street
Mittagong NSW 2575

Index